D1587193

WITHDRAWN FROM
BROMLEY LIBRARIES

Bromley Libraries

30128 80274 914 6

wild things

funky little clothes to sew

Kirsty Hartley

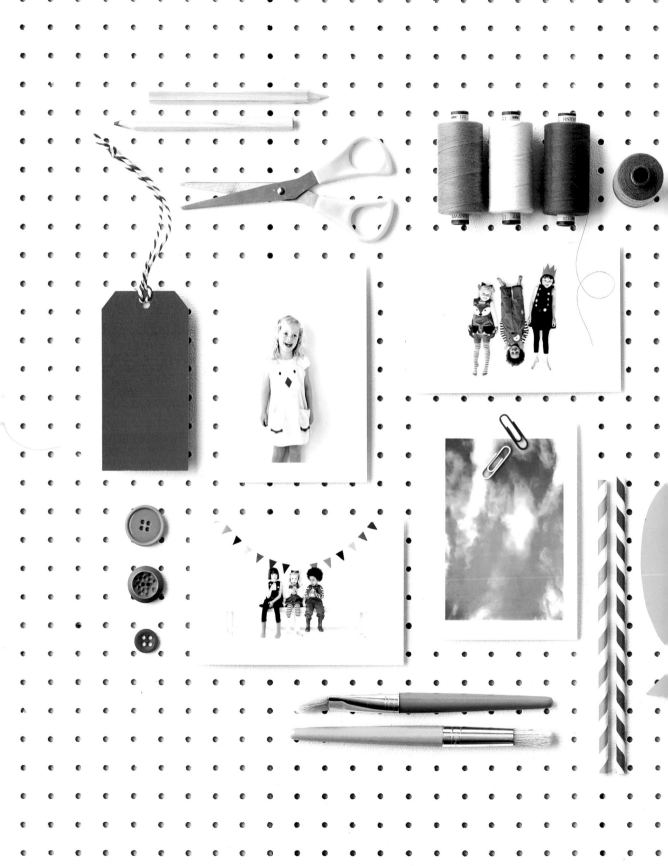

wild things

funky little clothes to sew

Kirsty Hartley

WEIDENFELD & NICOLSON

To my three Wild Things: Lila, Silva and Ewan for their boundless creative inspiration, love of life and imagination.

Contents

Introduction 6
Getting started 8
Useful materials and techniques 14
Measuring your child 30

DRESSES 34
    A-line dresses 36
    Sundresses and Rompers 76
    Apron dresses 96
    Long sleeved dresses 104

BOTTOMS 110
    Skirts 112
    Knickers and Bloomers 118

CHARACTER OUTFITS 128
    Dresses 130
    Dungarees 148
    Cape 168
    Jackets 174
    Hoodies 182
    Bonnet and Hats 190

Templates 196
Glossary 214
Index 216
Stockists 220

Introduction

As a mum of three juggling life in the heart of rural Lancashire with a career in fashion design and lecturing, I wanted to return to my roots. I've always been a prolific maker, so I revived my love of making by starting my brand Wild Things. I wanted to design pieces with heart and soul, and started with a few heirloom dresses for my girls, Silva and Lila (now our house models). I want to share with you some ideas your children will love and as a maker I want to share the joys and satisfaction of making something to treasure that inspires your creativity.

As a child of the seventies, everything I wore was handmade with practicality in mind. I started to sew from an early age as those (now dying) skills were passed down. It was my late grandma, Florence, who inspired me from an early age, with her huge walk-in wardrobe of gowns and hats, and a sewing box full of goodies, and of course my mum, who showed me (with much patience) how to use paper patterns at an early age. Now it's my children who inspire me.

This book offers an exciting range of clothes to make yourself, designed to live and play in, evoke a sense of fun, and inspire your little ones' imaginations. Influenced by Scandinavian shape and nostalgic references to childhood, the designs are simple, bold and playful, and loved by children and parents alike, making getting dressed altogether more enjoyable. The satisfaction of creating something handmade for your children is part of an age-old tradition that involves passing down techniques, reusing precious and sentimental fabrics, and creating lasting memories. To upcycle and reshape something that was once special is also a great way to reduce waste, while creating something truly unique. The styles I've created here have a simple, bold feel, which will add fun and colour to your little ones' wardrobes. However, don't forget the importance of choosing fabrics and trims that you love, to add a personalised charm to your items.

The beauty of the patterns (located in the envelope and on the web, see page 11), sized 6 months to 6 years, is their adaptability, providing you with a creative starting point for a whole new wardrobe of shapes. The templates (see page 196) also give you a range of inspiring imagery to work with, all of which can be mixed about to create endless unique items.

The book offers something for beginners to more advanced makers, and whatever your confidence level, the secret is to have a go and not to be too precious or precise; every piece has its own character and, with age, will take on a distinctive crafted feel.

Let these charming designs inspire your creativity to make simple heirlooms you'll treasure forever.

Kirsty xx

Getting started

INSPIRE

The aim of this little book is to inspire makers of all abilities to create something exciting that their children will really want to wear. Involve your children in the choices of colours, fabrics and imagery you use, and show them how it's coming along. With determination and a sense of achievement you'll hopefully achieve a spark in them to do the same!

As a child, my mum would dress me in her own creations, always in something ahead of the time. I also remember waiting with trepidation for birthday gifts from a much loved great-aunt, who enjoyed making everything, especially knitted granny squares. Who could have guessed that these would be enjoying such a revival today?

KIT

- Sewing machine, including an assortment of spare needles for use with different fabric weights
- Ironing board and a good-quality steam iron
- Fabric scissors – choose ones that you find comfortable to use
- Small craft scissors for detail work
- Seam ripper – a small, useful tool for unpicking seams
- Dressmaker's pins
- Sewing needles for hand work
- Tailor's chalk or erasable chalk pencil
- Large ruler or pattern cutting square
- Tape measure
- Space! You need room to think as well as to work – a clear dining table is ideal

ENJOY

The key is to have fun: take your time and enjoy what you do. Be prepared to make mistakes, but persevere! The techniques are deliberately simple; the aim is to get you started and not overwhelm with discipline. If you feel safest when following instructions, everything is here for you. If, on the other hand, you like to improvise and adapt, then this book provides an excellent starting point and a core of patterns for you to use and make your own. There are plenty of elements, such as the character faces, which you can mix and match with other styles and details to create your own pieces.

OVERCOME

When I ask new makers what their biggest hurdle is, they always say it's using their sewing machine. Overcome these battles by getting to know your machine; take a look at your user manual and make sure you know how to thread the machine, how to adjust the tension and stitch settings, and how to change a needle. Try out different stitches on a few scraps of fabric or – even better – ask a sewing friend to show you the ropes.

SPACE

Organise. Space to think and a clear workspace is really important, even if you have to pack everything away afterwards. The designs in this book are easy to work with because they're small, but having a clear flat space to cut out your patterns is really important.

FINISH

One thing I learned from my training as a dressmaker was the importance of a good finish. Press and prepare as you go along and make the smaller detailed parts first, keeping bigger pieces of fabric folded and ready. Don't over handle things and if you make a mistake don't despair; simply take a break, then unpick, press again and carry on.

NEW FROM OLD
Keep a box of special pieces of clothing and trims such as vintage buttons or appliqué to use for your projects. Add new life to old by upcycling, even if it's just a tiny detail. Adding something 'pre-loved' will give real charm and character to your clothes.

NOTE
All of the pieces are adaptable but I've provided templates at the back of the book to get you started. The patterns can be found in the envelope or to download on the web:

www.orionbooks.co.uk/ wtpatterns1 and
www.orionbooks.co.uk/ wtpatterns2

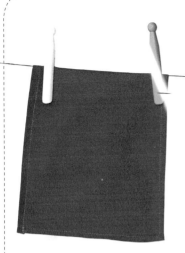
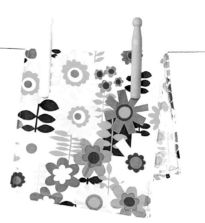

FABRIC

The sewing revival in recent years has seen traditional craft shops springing up and has brought forth a flurry of lovely online fabric stores, as well as inspirational blogs from talented stitchers offering inspiration, advice and sewing tutorials. Online fabric suppliers now offer a fantastic range of cotton-based fabrics, many of which can be bought in small quantities and delivered in next to no time. If you are lucky enough to have a fabric shop near you, take time to visit and familiarise yourself with the wealth of fabric constructions and fibres available. The projects in this book all have fabric suggestions (including amounts) to help you create something that is closely similar to the samples shown.

There are two basic types of fabric you can use for making clothes: woven or knitted. Woven fabrics are generally more stable to work with, especially if you are a beginner. Stretch fabrics such as jersey, interlock and fleece require a stitch setting on your sewing machine that will allow the seam to stretch with the garment and not 'crack'. Refer to your machine's user manual for more information, but generally a slight zigzag setting on a standard machine will work.

NOTE
Both metric and imperial measurements are given throughout this book. Please use one or the other for accuracy; this is particularly important when using quilter's cottons, which are sold as 'fat quarters' or quarter yards, cut to give a large quarter cut of the yard. You can also request a 'skinny quarter', which is cut across the entire width of the fabric. Buying in centimetres on the other hand can be a little more flexible, as buying in multiples of 10cm is often possible, giving a little less wastage.

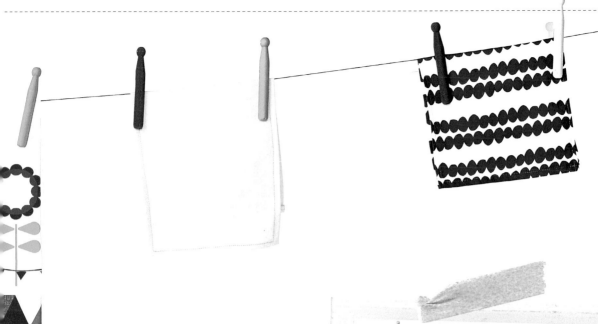

ONLINE

In an ever fast-moving world of technology and information, the need to 'switch off' and work with your hands to create something with a little soul has undoubtedly brought you to this stage. The key is to use the wealth of information at your fingertips to offer inspiration, as well as find simple solutions to ordering fabric and trims. Online magazines, blogs, and Etsy the 'world's handmade marketplace', review and promote amazing things makers like you have produced, as well as give an insight into skills and useful tips.

Useful Materials & Techniques

A story
to tell

Dick Bruna

APPLIQUÉ

This term comes from the French word for 'to apply'. In sewing it means adding a layer of fabric decoration to a larger piece of fabric. Traditionally appliqué would have involved intricate handwork using a paper design template and then hand sewing onto the main fabric. A simple alternative is to use a heat bonding appliqué paper, or iron-on, double-sided adhesive web, which is backed with paper on one side.

1. Draw or trace your design onto the paper backing, remembering it will appear in reverse on the right side of the fabric.

2. Cut out each shape.

3. Select a piece of fabric that is slightly larger than your design and use an iron to bond the design to the wrong side of the fabric, following the manufacturer's instructions.

4. Peel the paper backing from the appliqué fabric and assemble the design onto the main fabric, adhesive side down.

5. Use an iron to bond the appliqué pieces to the main fabric.

6. Use a sewing machine to stitch 2mm in from the edges of all the pieces to secure in place. This is known as edge stitching and is quick, easy and effective. After time and washing the result will be something with a lovely hand-crafted feel. You can also use heavyweight bonding web for a more permanent finish.

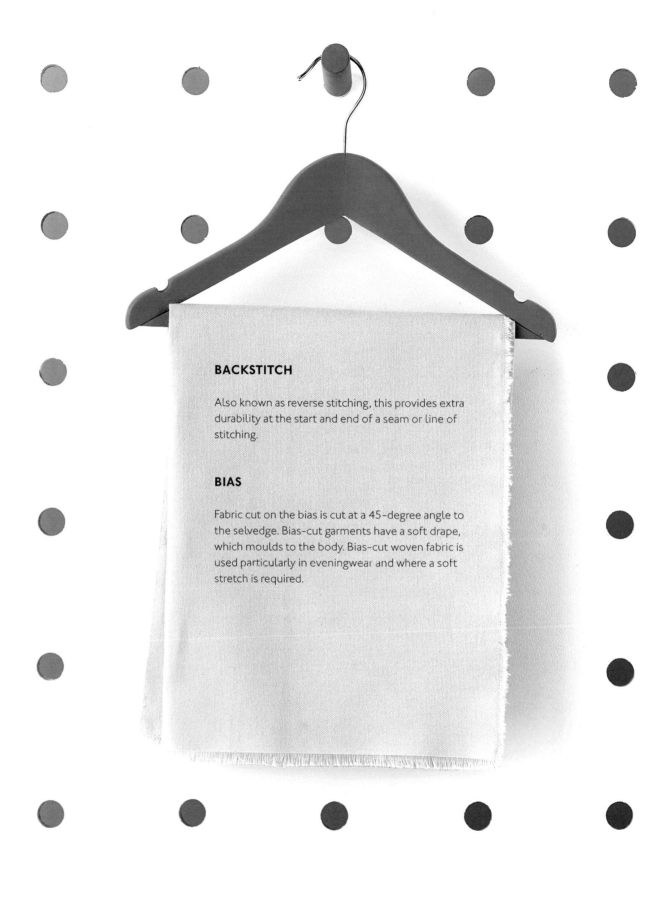

BACKSTITCH

Also known as reverse stitching, this provides extra durability at the start and end of a seam or line of stitching.

BIAS

Fabric cut on the bias is cut at a 45-degree angle to the selvedge. Bias-cut garments have a soft drape, which moulds to the body. Bias-cut woven fabric is used particularly in eveningwear and where a soft stretch is required.

BINDING

This is the technique of creating a decorative border to finish an edge, using pre-prepared or self-made fabric. Binding is cut from bias-cut fabric, making it an excellent finish for a curved edge.

1. Cut one strip (or several lengths) of fabric on the bias, at a 45-degree angle to the selvedge. To determine the width of the strips, decide on the depth of the binding you want, double this, then add seam allowances of 1cm (³/₈in). Heavyweight fabrics require more seam allowance, lightweight fabrics less. For a plain cotton fabric binding that is 1.5cm (⁵/₈in) wide, 5cm (2in) is a good guide.

2. Press both long edges in by 1cm (³/₈in).

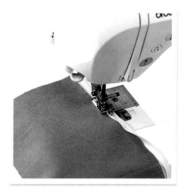

3. Then press the binding in half lengthways.

4. Unfold and place the right side of the binding to the wrong side of the edge you wish to finish, edges meeting. Sew along the folded line. Then press towards the edge.

5. Carefully fold back the binding and press. Fold the binding over the edge to the right side of the main fabric as desired.

6. Machine stitch the binding into place on the right side of the main fabric. This can be quite tricky, especially on curved edges, so take your time. You might wish to tack first and ease the binding into place as you work along the edge, taking care it doesn't twist or 'rope' as you go.

BUTTONS

To sew a button into place:

1. Mark your button position and thread your needle with a double thickness of thread.

2. Sew a single stitch back and forth in position to secure.

3. Sew through the holes or shank (the stem) in the button, then back through the fabric. Repeat several times.

4. If you are using a plain button as shown, create a mock shank or stem, so that the button sits neatly when fastened. Bring your needle to the face of the garment. You may wish to gently ease the button away from the fabric so that the stitching becomes looser. Then wrap the thread around the stitching several times to create the shank.

5. Finally sew through to the reverse and sew a few small stitches back and forth in position to secure. Cut the loose ends.

BUTTONHOLES

A basic buttonhole has a bar tack at each end and two sides, which are closely satin stitched. Refer to your sewing machine manual to select the correct setting. Practise on a scrap of similar weight fabric first. The fabric should be stable and able to take the weight of a heavy satin stitch without clogging. On some lightweight or open weave fabrics, you may require a small square of interfacing ironed onto the wrong side of the fabric. This will strengthen, especially if the button is likely to receive some wear and tear.

1. Mark your buttonhole top and bottom along the grain line.

2. Using matching sewing thread, follow the steps shown in your manual to complete the buttonhole as follows: left side, bottom, right side, top.

3. Using small sharp scissors or a seam ripper, carefully cut through the centre to create the buttonhole.

CUTTING

Choose cutting shears or scissors that are comfortable to hold, especially if you are left-handed, as I am. Use scissors with long blades for fabric cutting and a smaller pair for fine work or for trimming. Always press your fabric before cutting. Mark around your pattern with an erasable marker such as tailor's chalk on the reverse of the fabric. Note that these patterns require seam allowance.

Be sure to arrange the pattern pieces carefully before cutting, in order to maximise the use of your fabric. Observe the direction of any pile, nap or print direction, to ensure that ample allowance is left to add seam allowances. Always cut on a flat surface.

EASING

Easing involves gently allowing one longer seam to match another when sewing, by 'easing' it into place, usually when sewing curved or gathered edges. Start by matching both fabrics at the ends or between notches. Pin at 45 degrees to the edge, distributing the excess fabric evenly. Ease the two layers of fabric as you sew them together so that the seam line is smooth.

EDGE STITCHING

Stitching close to an edge secures appliqué or provides a neat finish.

FACING

This is an inner layer of fabric, cut to form a finished edge and strengthen the main body of a garment, for example on a jacket front. The Simple A-line dress on page 36 has a facing, which allows a neat finish of the neckline and armholes. Normally cut from self- or matching fabric, it may be backed with interfacing, if desired, to strengthen.

FAT QUARTER

A fat quarter refers to a quarter yard of quilting fabric, often quilter's cotton, measuring 45cm (18in) by 55cm (22in), assuming that the fabric is 110cm (44in) wide. Refer to each project for required fabric quantities, which are given in both metric and imperial.

FINISH

Technical accuracy is desirable, but not essential to achieve a good finish – careful pressing will make all the difference. (Finish also refers to any treatment on a fabric such as a coating or brush 'finish'.)

FOLD LINE

This refers to the marking on a pattern that requires you to place the pattern onto a folded piece of fabric, when the opposite side of the folded area is symmetrical.

FRENCH SEAM

This refers to a seam that is first sewn with wrong sides of fabric facing, then trimmed and pressed, then the process repeated with the right sides facing. It makes an ideal alternative finish to fine fabrics where you may see the seam inside and don't want to see overlocking.

GATHERING

To gather, first measure the length you wish to gather to. The simplest way to gather the edge of your fabric is to sew two parallel lines, one within the seam allowance and one just outside the seam allowance, lines approximately 5mm (¼in) apart. Use a long stitch setting so these gathering stitches can easily be removed. Secure one end of your stitching by backstitching. Now take the opposite loose ends and gently ease the fabric along the threads to gather the fabric to the required length. Sew the gathered fabric into place along the seam line. Remove the gather stitch if required.

GRAIN LINE

The grain line always runs parallel to the selvedge of a woven fabric. It is marked on the pattern piece as a long arrow, normally parallel to the centre front or centre back of the garment, or running lengthways down a sleeve. It indicates where to place the pattern on to the fabric.

HEMS

Normally a hem will be turned under once, then a second time to conceal any raw edges. Hems can be stitched into place by machine, or by hand using a slipstitch, or other hand hemming stitches.

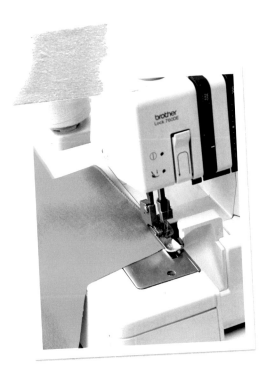

NOTCH

A notch is a mark on a pattern piece that denotes where it, and a corresponding notch on another pattern piece, are intended to be placed together – rather like a jigsaw puzzle. Transfer notches from the pattern to the fabric, and make a small nick within the seam allowance when you cut out the fabric to transfer the notch to all the pieces.

OVERLOCK

Overlocking is a necessary finish to the raw edges of fabric. Fully lined garments need not be overlocked. A specific overlock machine that will finish and trim simultaneously is ideal, although a zigzag stitch, or similar stitch setting on a standard sewing machine will suffice. Alternatively a French seam or bound seam will work just as well.

PILE AND NAP

The raised pile on a fabric such as velvet or corduroy lies in a clear direction. This means you need to cut everything with the pile running in the same direction and may need to allow extra fabric to do so. When cutting, the pile will generally run down the fabric.

PRESSING

Use a good quality steam iron and a clean ironing board cover. Alternatively, have a pressing cloth to hand to keep things clean and protected. Pressing seams open or to one side is essential to achieve a good finish, and you should do this as you go along. Generally press on the reverse to protect the fabric. Prevent a pile from flattening by pressing the piece face down on a scrap of the same fabric.

RAW EDGE

This is the unfinished edge of cut fabric.

RIGHT SIDES TOGETHER / RS FACING

This refers to when the face or right sides of fabric are placed together before sewing, so that the seam is hidden when the fabric is turned right side out. Wrong sides together means the opposite.

ROULEAU LOOP

A rouleau loop is made from bias-cut fabric and used to loop around a button to form a fastening. Take a bias-cut strip of fabric 8 × 3cm (3 × 1¼in). Fold lengthways, right sides together and stitch along one edge, leaving a long thread at the end. Carefully thread the loose thread through a large darning needle. Feed the needle back through the inside of the channel and carefully pull the fabric through to form the rouleau.

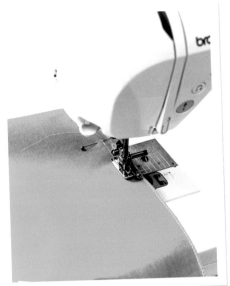

SEAM

A plain seam is achieved by placing two pieces of fabric right sides together and sewing a straight line, the required distance from the raw edge. The fabric from the seam line to the raw edge is called the seam allowance. In this book all the seam allowances are 1cm (³⁄₈in) unless otherwise specified. Pressing a seam open creates a neat finish. Other seam finishes such as welt, French, run and fell can also be used.

SELVEDGE

The selvedge is the finished edge of the fabric running down the edge (with the warp) of a woven fabric. The weft threads run across the width of the fabric.

SNIPPING CURVED EDGES AND CORNERS

Curved seam edges at armholes and necklines, for example, should be snipped carefully across the seam allowance, not too close to the seam itself, so that when turned through the edge remains curved. Likewise, corners should be trimmed by snipping across them at a 45-degree angle to reduce bulk when turned through.

TACK / BASTE

Hand sewing to temporarily secure layers into place is called tacking (basting) and helps with precision and fine work. Tacking threads are removed after sewing.

TOPSTITCH

Topstitching can be used for decorative purposes but more often it is used to achieve a flat and strong edge finish. It simply means stitching through one or more layers with the right side of the garment facing. For example a collar or a patch pocket might be topstitched.

ZIPS

The following is a guide to inserting a standard nylon zip.

1. Overlock all seams if the garment is unlined.

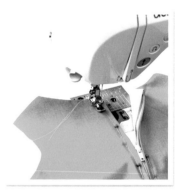

2. Mark the length of your zip along the opening from the top of the neckline downwards. Sew a seam up to this point.

3. Now press the seam open and continue to press the seam allowance open right to the top.

4. Pin your zip into position. It's also worth tacking the zip into place before you start. The aim is for the zip teeth to be covered by fabric.

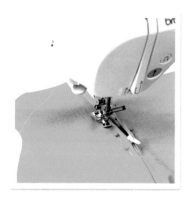

5. Referring to your sewing machine manual, select the correct setting and foot for your machine. A zipper foot allows you to sew closer to the teeth of the zip. Sew the zip into place an appropriate distance from the edge, approximately 5mm (¼in), depending on the weight of the fabric and the depth of your seam allowance.

6. You could hand stitch the facing into place around the zip. Alternatively, carefully machine stitch it into place by sewing over the original stitches, but this time through all layers to secure the lining in place.

Measuring your child

I have provided clothing sizes below, as guidelines, which are useful if your child isn't to hand. Measure your child's waist, chest and height to select the appropriate pattern size. The dress projects also include a guide for you to work out your required fabric lengths. For US quarter measurements, request thin quarters and not fat quarters to be cut from the bolt, so the fabric is cut as one continual length.

AVERAGE MEASUREMENTS BY AGE

AGE	HEIGHT	CHEST	WAIST
6–18 months	to 80cm (31½in)	to 50cm (20in)	to 46cm (18in)
18 months–3 years	to 98cm (39in)	to 54cm (22in)	to 50cm (20in)
3–5 years	to 110cm (43in)	to 58cm (23in)	to 54cm (22in)
5–7 years	to 122cm (48in)	to 63cm (25in)	to 58cm (23in)

*If the child you are creating the garment for is smaller or larger than average, you will need to adjust to fit.

A-LINE DRESS (SEE PAGE 36): FINISHED MEASUREMENTS

SIZE	LENGTH FROM SNP*	CHEST	HEM CIRCUMFERENCE
6–18 months	44cm (17½in)	55cm (22cm)	80cm (31½in)
18 months–3 years	49cm (19½in)	60cm (24in)	90cm (35½in)
3–5 years	55cm (22in)	66cm (26½in)	100cm (39½in)
5–7 years	62cm (24½in)	71cm (28½in)	110cm (43in)

*SNP – side neck point (measured from point on garment closest to neck)

CHARACTER DRESS (SEE PAGE 130): FINISHED MEASUREMENTS

SIZE	LENGTH FROM SNP*	CHEST
6–18 months	44cm (17½in)	58cm (23in)
18 months–3 years	49cm (19½in)	62cm (24½in)
3–5 years	55cm (22in)	68cm (27in)
5–7 years	62cm (24½in)	75cm (30in)

*SNP – side neck point (measured from point on garment closest to neck)

DUNGAREE (SEE PAGE 148): FINISHED MEASUREMENTS

SIZE	LENGTH (from underarm to hem extended)	HIP	HEIGHT OF CHILD
6–18 months	45cm (18in)	68cm (27in)	to 80cm (31in)
18 months–3 years	61cm (24½in)	76cm (30½in)	to 98cm (39in)
3–5 years	75cm (30in)	84cm (33½in)	to 110cm (43in)

1

Dresses

Simple A-line dress

This cool, retro A-line shape is perfect for bold funky prints. It's easy to wear on its own, or layered with bright tops and tights and finished off with a lovely pair of wellies. Play with colour – add contrast bindings, trims or pockets. You can choose to make the dress lined, or with simple neck and armhole facings.

YOU WILL NEED

- A-line dress and pocket patterns (follow the lines for a seamed shoulder)
- 1 length of dress fabric (see Calculating fabric lengths, below)
- 1 length of lining fabric (optional) (see Calculating fabric lengths, below)
- Tailor's chalk
- Contrast fabric for pockets, if desired
- 18cm (7in) matching zip (optional)
- Matching sewing thread

CUTTING OUT

Before you start, decide whether your dress will be lined, or have a simple faced neck and armhole. You can also choose to have a zip fastening at the back neck, or a simple keyhole opening, which works well for fabrics with large-scale patterns.

1. Choose the best size for your child, using the guide on page 30. Trace the pattern for the A-line dress in the envelope, following the lines for the correct size. Make a pattern for the front, with the neck sitting lower, and another for the back.

2. Press the fabric and arrange it on a flat surface so you can cut out one whole dress front and either one whole back or two separate back pieces. Make sure the grain lines on the pattern are parallel to the selvedge. If you are using printed fabric, take care that the direction of the pattern is the same for each piece.

3. Mark around the pattern pieces using tailor's chalk, adding 1cm (³/₈in) all around, but 2cm (³/₄in) at the hem. Cut the front and back pieces out carefully, still on a flat surface.

4. If you have chosen to make a zip fastening, cut the back of the dress in two halves, allowing for a 1cm (³/₈in) seam running down the centre back into which you will add the zip.

(CON'T)

CALCULATING FABRIC LENGTHS	6 months–3 years	3–7 years
Width 110cm (44in) lined dress *	70cm (27½in)	80cm (31½in)
Width 150cm (60in) lined dress *	70cm (27½in)	80cm (31½in)
Width 110cm (44in) dress with facing	1m (39in)	120cm (47in)
Width 150cm (60in) dress with facing	1m (39in)	120cm (47in)

* For the lined dress you will need the same amount of lining fabric.

5. To make the dress with facings to finish the neck edge and armholes, simply cut facing patterns by drawing a straight line across the body patterns (as marked), 4cm (1½in) below the armholes. The facing can be in the same fabric as the main dress or in a plain cotton.

6. To make a fully lined dress, you will need to cut a complete new dress from lining fabric. The lining dress should be at least 2cm (¾in) shorter in length. The rest of the instructions are given for the version above, with facings, but the method for the lined dress is the same.

POCKETS

1. Cut out either one or two pockets, using the pattern provided.

2. Overlock the edges and press them under by 1cm (⅜in). Overlocking is not essential, but prevents the pockets from fraying on the inside.

3. Fold the top of the pocket back twice by 1cm (⅜in) and press. Topstitch to secure.

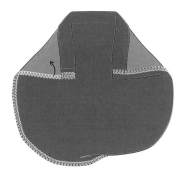

4. Place the pocket in position on the dress front as required and pin. Topstitch around the side and bottom edges, backstitching at the start and finish to secure. You may wish to add a small triangular shape of stitching at each top corner to make the opening extra secure.

TIP
Experiment with contrast pockets (see page 19): if you are using a printed fabric, self-fabric pockets can often become lost, so choose something that contrasts but complements at the same time.

SEWING FACINGS

1. Place the front facing, (or lining) and the dress front right sides together, pin, and sew around the neck and armhole openings.

2. Carefully snip the curved edges, to within 2mm from the seam. This releases the seam on the inside and will give a good curved finish.

3. Turn through carefully and press.

4. Repeat for the back of the dress, following the instructions on pages 40–41 for either a keyhole back or a zipped back.

(CON'T)

OPTION A
KEYHOLE BACK

1. Place the back facing (or lining) and the dress back right sides together and pin into place. Mark the keyhole position with chalk or a pencil.

2. Carefully mark the stitch line for the keyhole opening, to create a neat symmetrical curve at the bottom end when turned through.

3. Prepare a rouleau loop from the main fabric by cutting an 8 × 3cm (3 × 1¼in) bias strip. Fold, right sides together, and sew along one edge, leaving a long thread at the end. Thread the loose threads at the end through a large darning needle. Feed the needle back through the inside of the channel, and carefully pull the fabric through to form the rouleau.

4. Fold the rouleau to make a loop and pin it in position at the neck, opening between the dress back and the facing (or lining) and pin into place. The loop should be large enough to comfortably fit around the button you wish to use. Trim if necessary. Sew around the armholes and neckline as for the front, creating the keyhole shape as you go.

5. Carefully cut down the centre back to create the keyhole opening and trim back the edges to create a neat curve when turned through. Turn through carefully and press.

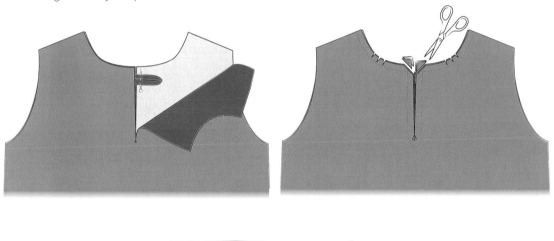

OPTION B
ZIPPED BACK

There are a number of ways to insert a zip, but I find this method works well for woven fabrics. See page 29 for more detail. Experienced sewers may have a variation they prefer.

1. You will have the main fabric for the back cut into two halves. Overlock the centre back edges and place right sides together. Mark the length of your zip along the opening from the top of the neckline downwards. Sew a seam from the bottom of the dress up to this point.

2. Now press the seam open and continue to press the seam allowance right to the top.

3. Pin your zip into position. The aim is for the zip teeth to be covered by fabric. It's worth tacking the zip into place before you start.

4. Following your sewing machine manual, select the correct setting and foot to sew the zip into place, 5mm (¼in) from the edge.

5. Now repeat steps 1 and 2 by sewing the centre back of the facing (or lining).

6. Place the dress back and the facing right sides together and sew around the neckline and armholes. Carefully clip the curved edges to give a neat finish. Turn through and press.

7. To sew the facing (or lining) into place around the zip, you may hand stitch, or carefully machine stitch into place by sewing over the original stitches, working with the right side of the dress, but this time through all layers to secure the lining into place. If required, pin first with the pins positioned horizontally, but take care not to sew over a pin.

(CON'T)

JOINING

1. Place the turned-through dress front and dress back right sides of the main fabric together, matching the shoulder seams so all four shoulder edges meet, as shown in the illustration. Sew the four layers of fabric together 1cm (³/₈in) from the edge at the shoulder point.

2. Pin the side seams, right sides of the dress and rights side of the facing (or lining) together, carefully matching at the armhole seam. Sew and press. Overlock raw edged as required.

3. Turn the dress to the right side and topstitch around the neck and armholes, 1cm (³/₈in) from the edge. Press.

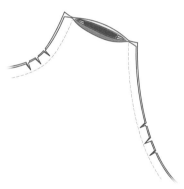

FINISHING

1. Finish the hem edge by turning 1cm (³/₈in), then another 1cm (³/₈in) to the wrong side and stitching down. You can stitch the hem by hand if you prefer.

2. Topstitch around the arm and neck edges, 5mm (¹/₄in) from the edges, taking care at the curved edges. This will give a neat finish.

3. If you chose the keyhole opening option, sew a button into place.

TIP
For added detail, topstitch in contrast thread or use a fun button. If you would like to add a contrast edge to the hemline, see the instructions on page 47.

Reversible pinny with pockets

The dress is reversible, so it's very useful, and there is no need to finish seams on the inside. The cool retro A-line shape is a perfect starting point for a simple appliqué graphic, or for one of those funky prints that are so easy to find online. The dress fastens on the shoulders with a clever double button fastening. Treat it as a blank canvas and let your imagination inspire you.

YOU WILL NEED

- A-line dress and pouch patterns (follow the lines marked for a button shoulder fastening)
- 2 × lengths of dress fabric (see Calculating fabric lengths, below)
- Contrast fabric for pockets, if desired
- Tailor's chalk
- Matching sewing threads
- 30cm (12in) square of iron-on, double-sided adhesive web
- 4 buttons, 2cm (3⁄4in) diameter (these will form a double button fastening)

CUTTING OUT

1. Choose the best size for your child, using the guide on page 30. Trace the pattern for the A-line dress in the envelope, following the lines for the correct size. Make a pattern for the front, with the neck sitting lower, and another for the back.

2. Press the fabric and arrange it on a flat surface so you can cut out one whole dress front and one whole back. Make sure the centre front and centre back are parallel to the selvedge.

3. Mark around the pattern pieces using tailor's chalk, adding 1cm (3⁄8in) all around, but 2cm (3⁄4in) at the hem. Cut the pieces out carefully.

4. Repeat steps 1–3 for the reverse fabric, so you have two fronts and two backs.

(CON'T)

CALCULATING FABRIC LENGTHS	6 months–3 years	3–7 years
Width 110cm (44in) lined dress *	70cm (27 1⁄2 in)	80cm (31 1⁄2 in)
Width 150cm (60in) lined dress *	70cm (27 1⁄2 in)	80cm (31 1⁄2 in)

* For the lined dress you will need the same amount of lining fabric.

POCKETS

1. In a contrast fabric, cut a large pouch pocket for one side, and a smaller one, if you choose, for the reverse, using the pattern as a guide.

2. Overlock the edges (not essential) and press them under by 1cm (³⁄₈in).

3. Fold the top of the pocket back twice by 1cm (³⁄₈in) and press. Topstitch to secure.

4. Place the pockets in position on each of the front dress pieces as required and pin. Topstitch around the side and bottom edges, backstitching at the start and finish to secure.

5. To decorate the dress, if you have a large-scale print, select a motif to use, and back it with the adhesive web. Cut out the shape and peel the paper backing from the reverse. Position it just above the pocket to the side, press, then topstitch around the edges to secure.

> **TIP**
> Why not look at some of the designs and motifs used on pockets throughout the book and create your own version? If you wish to have two gathered pockets, see the instructions on page 50.

SEWING SEAMS AND JOINING

1. Place the dress front and back right sides together and sew down one side only, sewing 1cm (³⁄₈in) from the edge. Press the seam open.

2. Sew one seam on the reverse dress in the same way, making sure the seam will go with the seam already sewn in the main dress. Press the seam open.

3. On a flat surface, carefully place the two dresses right sides together and pin around the entire upper edge around the neck, armholes and across the shoulders. Tack if desired. Sew 1cm (³⁄₈in) from the edge. Sewing around the curved edges can be tricky, so take your time, gently rotating the fabric as you go, with the needle in the fabric and the machine foot raised. (Always sew with the foot down in position.)

4. Carefully snip the curved edges, to within 2mm of the seam. This releases the seam on the inside and gives a good curved finish. Snip excess fabric from the corners of the straps.

5. Turn through carefully and press.

6. Sew the remaining open sides of the main dress, placing right sides of fabric together. Press the seams open and reverse the dress.

FINISHING

1. Topstitch around the arm and neck edges 5mm (¼in) from the edge, taking care around the curves. Lay the dress flat and press.

2. Sew one buttonhole on each strap on the back of the dress. Practise first and refer to your sewing machine manual for guidance.

3. Sew two buttons into place on each front strap, one on the face and one on the reverse. If you can, sew buttons on both sides at the same time!

4. You can now finish the hem in one of two ways (see below):

OPTION A

Press the bottom edge of each dress back by 1cm (⅜in). Place these edges together with the raw edges on the inside, pin and carefully sew together 5mm (²/8in) from the edge.

OPTION B
CREATE A CONTRAST TURNING ON ONE SIDE

Lay the dress flat and trim the hem edges to the same length if necessary. Tack the hem edges together, then press back twice to form a 1cm (⅜in) deep hem. You will have a contrast hem on one side of the dress. Topstitch in place.

Rainbow dress

This cheerful dress is all about adding a splash of colour. Choose a neutral sky tone if you can for the main fabric to give contrast to the bright rainbow – denim works well.

YOU WILL NEED

- A-line dress and pocket patterns (follow the lines marked for a button shoulder fastening)
- 1 length of dress fabric (see Calculating fabric lengths, below)
- Assorted fabric scraps for the appliqué rainbow, clouds and raindrops
- Tailor's chalk
- Sewing threads
- Iron-on, double-sided adhesive web
- 2 chunky buttons approximately (2.5cm/1in) diameter
- 20cm (8in) × 50mm (¼ inch) wide elastic

CUTTING OUT

1. Choose the best size for your child, using the guide on page 30. Trace the pattern for the A-line dress in the envelope, following the lines for the correct size. Make a pattern for the front, with the neck sitting lower, and another for the back.

2. Press the fabric and arrange it on a flat surface so you can cut out one whole dress front, one whole back, matching facings and one pocket. Make sure the centre front and centre back are parallel to the selvedge. If you are using a fabric with a pile such as velvet or corduroy, remember to cut the pieces with the pile running downwards for all pieces.

3. Mark around the pattern pieces using tailor's chalk, adding 1cm (³⁄₈in) all around, but 2cm (¾in) at the hem. Cut the pieces out carefully.

(CON'T)

CALCULATING FABRIC LENGTHS	6 months–3 years	3–7 years
Width 110cm (44in) dress with facings	1m (39in)	120cm (47in)
Width 150cm (60in) dress with facings	1m (39in)	120cm (47in)

POCKET

1. Prepare the pocket by overlocking the edges. Fold and press back the curved edge by 1cm (³/₈in).

2. Fold back the top edge by 1.5cm (⁵/₈in). Sew the edge down, making a channel through which to thread the elastic. Press.

3. Attach a safety pin to one end of the elastic and thread it through the channel at one end. Gently pull the elastic to create a gathered top. Secure by sewing the elastic at the other end. Pin and then topstitch the pocket into place on the dress close to the edge.

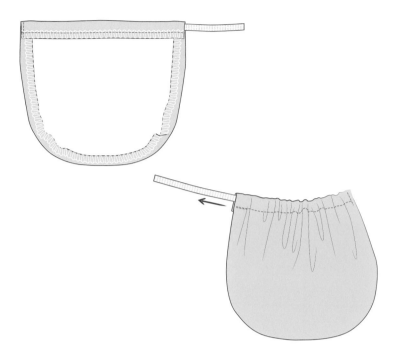

APPLIQUÉ

1. Prepare your appliqué fabrics by ironing the adhesive web to the wrong side. Turn them right side up and use the templates on pages 196 and 200 to draw the shapes on the fabric. Cut out the rainbow, numbering the stripes as you go on the wrong side. Cut the cloud and raindrops. I've used a metallic fabric for this dress so the appliqué really stands out.

2. Arrange the appliqué pieces into position on the dress panels, removing the paper backing adhesive side down. Use the photograph on page 48 as a guide. Take care to position the rainbow stripes accurately, so that when the side seam is sewn they are correctly aligned on the front and back of the dress.

3. Cover the fabric with a cloth and press the appliqué with an iron to bond the fabric.

4. Stitch around the edges of the appliqué pieces, using matching or contrast thread.

SEWING SEAMS AND JOINING

1. Assemble the dress by placing the dress front and back right sides together. Sew the side seam that joins the rainbow, 1cm (³/₈in) from the edge. Take care to align the rainbow appliqué stripes. Overlock the seam and press open.

2. Assemble and sew one seam on the facings, making sure it will go with the seam sewn on the main dress. Overlock and press open. Finish the lower edge: you can either turn it back by 5mm (¹/₄in) twice to create a rolled hem, or simply overlock.

3. Lay the dress on a flat surface, right side up. Place the facing on the dress right sides together. Pin the facing and dress together around the neck, armholes and across the shoulders. Sew 5mm (¹/₄in) from edge. Snip into the curves and across the excess at corners, taking care not to snip through the stitching itself.

4. Now sew the remaining side seams on the dress and facing.

5. Turn through, rolling fabric gently in places to shape the curved edges. Press, then topstitch 5mm (¹/₄in) from the edge around the armholes and neckline.

FINISHING

1. Hem the dress by turning the bottom edge back twice.

2. Mark the position of the buttonholes and then stitch, using the buttonhole setting on your sewing machine. Finish by cutting through the buttonhole centre with small, sharp scissors. Sew the buttons into place.

Flowerpot pinafore

This simple pinafore has a big pocket to stash little things while on the go. You can follow this design or create your own combination of colours and patterns. Simple flat, bright colours work well, but you can also try using tiny all-over prints. This is a great way to upcycle and incorporate pieces of treasured old clothing.

I love this little design as it has a real early-seventies feel to it. Using a medium- to heavyweight fabric gives the A-line shape a real kick.

YOU WILL NEED

- A-line dress pattern (follow the lines marked for a button shoulder fastening)
- 1 length of dress fabric (see Calculating fabric lengths, below)
- Contrast cotton fabric for facings (optional)
- 30cm (12in) square of fabric for the pocket
- 30cm (12in) square of iron-on, double-sided adhesive web
- Contrast fabric for the flower (plain or patterned)
- 2 chunky buttons, approximately 2.5cm (1in) diameter
- Matching sewing thread

CUTTING OUT

1. Choose the best size for your child, using the guide on page 30. Trace the pattern for the A-line dress in the envelope, following the lines for the correct size. Make a pattern for the front, with the neck sitting lower, and another for the back.

2. Press the fabric and arrange it on a flat surface so you can cut out one whole dress front, one whole back and matching facings. Make sure the centre front and centre back are parallel to the selvedge.

3. Mark around the pattern pieces using tailor's chalk, adding 1cm (³⁄₈in) all around, but 2cm (³⁄₄ in) at the hem. Cut the pieces out carefully.

(CON'T)

CALCULATING FABRIC LENGTHS	6 months–3 years	3–7 years
Width 110cm (44in) lined dress *	70cm (27½in)	80cm (31½in)
Width 150cm (60in) lined dress *	70cm (27½in)	80cm (31½in)
Width 110cm (44in) dress with facing	1m (39in)	120cm (47in)
Width 150cm (60in) dress with facing	1m (39in)	120cm (47in)

* For the lined dress you will also need the same amount of lining fabric.

POCKET AND APPLIQUÉ

1. Cut out the pocket. Use the template on page 197 adding 2cm (³⁄₄in)to the top of the pot, and 1cm around the other sides.

2. Cut out the flower template on page 197.

3. Gather the flower appliqué fabrics that you have chosen for your design and prepare them by ironing adhesive web to the wrong side of the scraps. Turn them right side up and use the templates to draw the shapes on the fabric. Cut out the flower, leaves and stem shapes.

4. Overlock the pocket sides and edges and turn the bottom under by 1cm (³⁄₈in).

5. Turn under the top of the pocket by 2cm (³⁄₄in). Stitch the top of the pocket into place, 1.5cm (⁵⁄₈in) from the edge.

6. To make it sturdier, back the pocket with a cotton calico or double the fabric. You can cut the pocket double by placing the top edge of the pocket onto folded fabric. This way there is no need to finish the pocket top separately.

7. Arrange the flower pieces into position on the front dress panel removing the paper backing, adhesive side down. Cover with a cloth and press to bond.

8. Stitch around the edges of the flower, using matching or contrast sewing thread.

9. Place the flowerpot pocket in place, pin and stitch very close to the side and bottom edges, making sure you start and finish with a backstitch to secure, or reinforce with triangles, as shown.

SEWING SEAMS AND JOINING

1. Assemble the dress by placing the dress front and back right sides together. Sew one side seam 1 cm (³⁄₈in) from the edge. Overlock this seam and press open. Place down flat, right side up.

2. Assemble and sew one seam on the facings (or lining), making sure it will go with the seam sewn on the main dress. Overlock and press open. Finish the lower edge: you can either turn it back by 5mm (¹⁄₄in) twice to create a rolled hem, or simply overlock.

3. Place the facing (or lining) on the dress right sides together. Pin the facing and dress together around the neck, armholes and across the shoulders. Sew 5mm (¹⁄₄in) from edge. Snip into the curves and across the excess at corners, taking care not to snip through the stitching itself.

4. Now sew the remaining side seams on the dress and facing (or lining) together. Overlock and press.

5. Turn through, rolling fabric gently in places to shape the curved edges. Press, then topstitch 5mm (¹⁄₄in) from edge, around the armholes and neckline.

FINISHING

1. Hem the dress by turning the bottom edge back twice by 1cm (³⁄₈in).

2. Mark the position of the buttonholes and then stitch, using the buttonhole setting on your sewing machine. Finish by cutting through the buttonhole centre with small, sharp scissors. Sew the buttons into place.

Flower collar dress

This adorable little dress lets your child dress as a flower. I love this style as it's a starting point for sharing nature with your little one. Again, it's my take on a sixties classic. I've chosen colour-popping shades, but it works well with pretty pastels and small prints too. Choose a medium-weight fabric, such as cotton twill or canvas, as it will give the dress shape a real sixties feel. You can also try cutting the dress a little shorter and make a simple cropped bloomer to wear underneath (see page 120). Perfect for special summer parties!

YOU WILL NEED

- A-line dress, pocket and collar patterns (following the cutting lines for a seamed shoulder)
- 1 length of dress fabric (see Calculating fabric lengths, below)
- Tailor's chalk
- Approximately 30cm (12in) square of green or contrast fabric for the stem and leaves
- 30cm (12in) square of iron-on, double-sided adhesive web
- 25cm (10in) or 1 fat quarter of bright cotton fabric for the collar
- 25cm (10in) square iron-on interfacing (optional)
- Matching sewing threads
- 1 button for the back neck

CUTTING OUT

1. Choose the best size for your child, using the guide on page 30. Trace the pattern for the A-line dress in the envelope, following the lines for the correct size. Make a pattern for the front, with the neck sitting lower, and another for the back.

2. Press the fabric and arrange it on a flat surface so you can cut out one whole dress front and two separate back pieces. Make sure the centre front and the centre back are parallel to the selvedge. This will allow you to add the collar and finish the neckline comfortably (these instructions follow slightly different stages from the Simple A-line dress.)

3. Mark around the pattern pieces using tailor's chalk, adding 1cm (3/8in) all around, but 2cm (3/4 in) at the hem. Cut the pieces out carefully.

(CON'T)

CALCULATING FABRIC LENGTHS	6 months–3 years	3–7 years
Width 110cm (44in) lined dress *	70cm (27½in)	80cm (31½in)
Width 150cm (60in) lined dress *	70cm (27½in)	80cm (31½in)
Width 110cm (44in) dress with facing	1m (39in)	120cm (47in)
Width 150cm (60in) dress with facing	1m (39in)	120cm (47in)

* For the lined dress you will also need the same amount of lining fabric.

4. To make this dress with facings, simply cut them from the same fabric as the main dress or from plain cotton by following the main patterns, 4cm (1 ½in) below the armholes.

5. To make a fully lined dress you will need to cut a complete new dress in lining fabric, but at least 2cm (¾in) shorter in length.

POCKET (IF REQUIRED)

1. Cut the pocket and overlock the edges (not essential). Press the curved edges under by 1cm (⅜in).

2. Fold the pocket top back twice and press. Sew to secure.

3. Place the pocket in position on the dress front as required and pin. Topstitch around the side and bottom edges, backstitching at start and finish to secure.

EMBELLISHING

1. Prepare the green fabric for the stem with the iron-on, double-sided adhesive web. Cut out several strips, 5–7mm (¼in) to create the stem, and several leaves. You could use the raindrop template as a guide for the leaves (see page 200).

2. Carefully draw a curved line from neck to hem on the dress front in tailor's chalk. Remove the paper backing from the green fabric strips and press over this line, gently easing to the shape of the curved line as you apply and joining together to create a continuous line. Topstitch the stem in place.

3. Position the leaves in the same way, press and topstitch them in place, close to the edge.

COLLAR AND NECKLINE

1. Cut two collars (the right side and a facing) from cotton fabric using the flower collar pattern on the web. It is unlikely you will need to strengthen the collar as it is simply for decoration; however, if you do, press an iron-on interfacing to the reverse of the collar facing.

2. Place the pieces right sides together and sew around the curved outer edges of the collar.

3. Snip into the curves to create a smooth, curved scalloped edge when turned back through. Turn through.

4. Press, then topstitch the outer edge 5mm (¼in) from the edge.

5. Place the front and back of the dress right sides together and sew the shoulder seams 1cm (³/₈in) from the edge. Press the seams open. Repeat for the facings (or lining).

6. Pin the collar in position around the neck of the dress, right sides together, leaving a 1cm (³/₈in) seam allowance at the centre back. Sew into position.

7. Now place the facing (or lining) onto the dress, right sides together, and sew around the neckline. Repeat for the armholes, taking care not to catch the collar into the seam. It may help to roll the collar a little so it doesn't get in the way when you're sewing. Snip into the curves around the neckline and the armholes. Turn the dress through.

(CON'T)

SEWING SEAMS AND JOINING

1. Overlock all the remaining raw edges.

2. Mark the length of the back neck opening from the top of the neckline down the centre back of the dress by approximately 8cm (3in). Place the back pieces right sides together and sew a seam from the hemline to this point. Press the seam open and continue to press up the neck for the slash neck opening. Repeat for the facing (or lining).

3. Prepare a rouleau loop from the main fabric (see Option A for the Simple A-line dress on page 40). Fold the rouleau to make a loop and pin it in position at the neck opening. The loop should be large enough to comfortably fit around your button. Finish the neck opening by pinning the dress and facing (or lining) together. Then topstitch close to the edge all the way around the opening.

4. Pin the side seams, right sides of the dress and rights side of the facing (or lining) together, carefully matching at the armhole seam. Sew and press.

FINISHING

1. Turn and sew a double hem of 1cm (³/₈in).

2. Carefully topstitch around the arm and neck edges 5mm (¹/₄in) from the edge.

3. Sew the button into place.

Happy landscape dress

This dress allows you to create a landscape that wraps around the dress. Make a copy of the A-line dress pattern as a starting point and then draw your design directly onto the pattern. Use this as a template for the shapes you have drawn to be appliquéd onto the dress. Why not let your little girl help you do this? Children's drawings are a perfect, simple starting point.

YOU WILL NEED

- A-line dress pattern (follow the lines marked for a button shoulder fastening)
- 1 length of dress fabric (see Calculating fabric lengths, below): choose a blue/grey colour if you can in a medium-weight fabric, such as canvas or twill, so the dress holds its A-line shape well
- Contrast fabrics for the landscape appliqué
- Iron-on double-sided adhesive web, enough to back your landscape fabrics
- 2 chunky buttons
- Matching sewing threads
- Tailor's chalk

CUTTING OUT

1. Choose the best size for your child, using the guide on page 30. Trace the pattern for the A-line dress in the envelope, following the lines for the correct size. Make a pattern for the front, with the neck sitting lower, and another for the back.

2. Press the fabric and arrange it on a flat surface so you can cut out one whole dress front, one whole back and matching facings. Make sure the centre front and centre back are parallel to the selvedge.

3. Mark around the pattern pieces using tailor's chalk, adding 1 cm ($^3/_8$in) all around, but 2 cm ($^3/_4$ in) at the hem. Cut the pieces out carefully.

(CON'T)

CALCULATING FABRIC LENGTHS	6 months–3 years	3–7 years
Width 110cm (44in) dress with facings	1m (39in)	120cm (47in)
Width 150cm (60in) dress with facings	1m (39in)	120cm (47in)

APPLIQUÉ

1. Draw your appliqué design onto the pattern; if you want to create a design that runs all around the dress, remember to make your lines match at the seams. Position the paper patterns side by side to do this.

2. Trace each shape, giving it a number or name, so that you can re-piece the design together later. Alternatively you can use the templates (see page 198).

3. Prepare the appliqué fabrics by ironing the adhesive to the reverse of the scraps. Turn them right side up, position the templates on top and mark around them. Cut out the shapes.

4. Peeling off the paper backing, position the appliqué pieces on the dress panels. Cover with a cloth and press with a moderate heat. For the lower landscape area you could also turn back the top edge, press and pin and sew into place. This will reduce the bulk of bonding adhesive in this area.

5. Topstitch around the edges of the appliqué using matching or contrast thread.

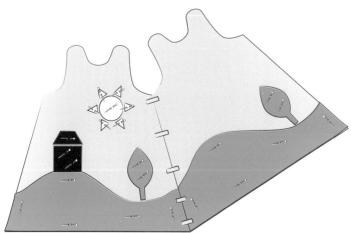

SEWING SEAMS AND JOINING

1. Assemble the dress by placing the dress front and back with right sides together. Sew one seam only, with a 1cm ($^3/_8$in) seam allowance. Overlock this seam and press. Open the dress and place on a flat surface, right side up.

2. Assemble and sew the facings at the opposite side seam only and open them out flat. Finish the lower edge by either turning back by 5mm ($^1/_4$in) twice, or simply overlocking.

3. Place the prepared facing onto the dress right sides together. Pin and sew into place 1cm ($^3/_8$in) from the outer edges. Snip into the curves, taking care not to snip through the stitching itself.

4. Now sew the remaining side seam and facing right sides together.

5. Turn through, rolling the fabric gently in places to shape the curved edges. Press, then topstitch 5mm ($^1/_4$in) around the top edges.

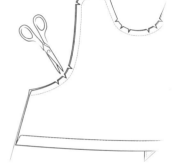

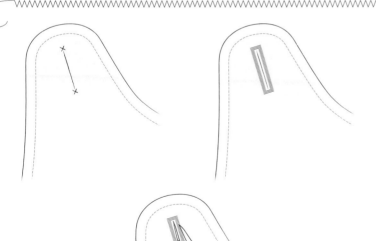

FINISHING

1. Hem the dress by turning 1cm ($^3/_8$in) back twice.

2. Mark the position of the buttonholes, then refer to your sewing machine manual to stitch them. Finish by cutting through the buttonhole centres with small sharp scissors.

3. Finally, sew the buttons into place.

Little Missy dress

This dress is a cheeky take on the A-line dress. The styling harks back to my childhood days. The mock buttons can also be used to create a lovely string of beads, which can be made in a whole host of fabrics. Perfect for dressing up like mum.

YOU WILL NEED

- A-line dress and collar patterns (following the marked lines for a seamed shoulder)
- 1 length of fabric (see Calculating fabric lengths, below): I've used cotton corduroy, but this dress works well in velvet or special fabrics
- Selection of small pieces of fabric for the mock buttons (or pearls)
- Iron-on, double-sided adhesive web
- 25cm (10in) or one fat quarter of bright fabric for the collar
- Matching sewing threads
- Tailor's chalk
- 18cm (7in) zip (optional)
- Button for back neck (optional)

CUTTING OUT

1. Choose the best size for your child, using the guide on page 30. Trace the pattern for the A-line dress in the envelope, following the lines for the correct size. Make a pattern for the front, with the neck sitting lower, and another for the back.

2. Press the fabric and arrange it on a flat surface so you can cut out one whole dress front and two separate back pieces. Make sure the centre front and the centre back are parallel to the selvedge.

3. Mark around the pattern pieces using tailor's chalk, adding 1cm ($^3/_8$in) all around, but 2cm ($^3/_4$ in) at the hem. Cut the pieces out carefully.

4. To make this dress with facings around the neck and armholes, simply cut them from the same fabric as the main dress or from plain cotton by following the main patterns, 4cm (1 $^1/_2$in) below the armholes.

5. To make a fully lined dress you will need to cut a complete new dress in lining fabric, at least 2cm ($^3/_4$in) shorter in length.

(CON'T)

CALCULATING FABRIC LENGTHS	6 months–3 years	3–7 years
Width 110cm (44in) lined dress *	70cm (27 $^1/_2$in)	80cm (31 $^1/_2$in)
Width 150cm (60in) lined dress *	70cm (27 $^1/_2$in)	80cm (31 $^1/_2$in)
Width 110cm (44in) dress with facing	1m (39in)	120cm (47in)
Width 150cm (60in) dress with facing	1m (39in)	120cm (47in)

* For the lined dress you will also need the same amount of lining fabric.

EMBELLISHING

Embellish the front of the dress, before sewing any of the dress pieces together. Work on a flat surface. Cut circles from bright coloured fabric that has been bonded on the reverse with iron-on adhesive web. Arrange these as buttons or beads, peel off the backing paper, then heat press them into place. Stitch down by either sewing a cross shape through the centre of each circle or sewing around the outer edge of the circle.

COLLAR AND NECKLINE

1. Cut two collars (the right side and the facing), using the collar pattern on the web (see page 11). The pattern is for the left only, and should be flipped over to make the right collar. It is unlikely you will need to strengthen the collar as it is simply for decoration; however, if you do, press an iron-on interfacing to the reverse of the collar facing.

2. Place the pieces right sides together and sew around the curved outer edges of the collar.

3. Snip into the curves to create a smooth, curved edge when turned back through. Turn through.

4. Press, then topstitch the outer edge 5mm (¹/₄in) from the edge.

5. Place the front and back of the dress right sides together and sew the shoulder seams 1cm (³/₈in) from the edge. Press the seams open. Repeat for the facings (or lining).

6. Pin the two prepared collar pieces on to the dress, facing side to the right side of the dress, working from the centre of the neck outwards. Note the collar shape is different at the back than the front, so be sure you are positioning the pieces correctly. Sew into position.

7. Now place the facing (or lining) onto the dress right sides together and sew around the neckline, trapping the collar within. Repeat for the armholes, taking care not to catch the collar into the seam. It may help to roll the collar a little so it doesn't get in the way when you're sewing. Snip into the curves around the neckline and the armholes. Turn the dress through and press.

(CON'T)

SEWING SEAMS AND JOINING

1. Overlock all the remaining raw edges.

2. On the main dress, mark the length of your zip or neck opening of 8cm (3in) from the top of the neckline down the back. Sew a seam from the hemline to this point. Press the seam open, continuing to press right to the neck. Repeat for the facing (or lining). Follow the instructions below for either a zipped back or a simple opening.

OPTION A
ZIPPED BACK

(See how to insert a zip on page 29.)

1. Pin your zip into position. It's worth tacking the zip into place before you start. The aim is for the zip teeth to be covered by fabric.

2. Following your sewing machine manual, select the correct setting and foot to sew the zip into place, 5mm (¼in) from the edge.

3. To sew the facing (or lining) into place around the zip, you may hand stitch, or carefully machine stitch it into place by sewing over the original stitches, but this time through all layers.

OPTION B
SIMPLE OPENING

1. Prepare a rouleau loop from the main fabric (see Option A for the Simple A-line dress on page 40). Fold the rouleau to make a loop and pin it in position at the neck opening. The loop should be large enough to comfortably fit around your button.

3. Complete the neck opening by sewing the dress fabric and facing (or lining) 2mm (⅛in) from the edge, all the way around the opening.

4. Sew a button in place at the top of the opening.

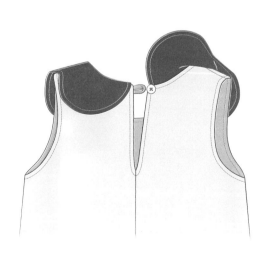

FINISHING

1. Pin the side seams, right sides of the dress and rights side of the facing (or lining) together, carefully matching at the armhole seam. Sew and press.

2. Finish the hem edge by turning back 1cm (3/8in) twice and stitching it in place.

3. Carefully topstitch around the arm and neck edges 5mm (1/4in) from the edge.

Carousel dress

A brave little party dress full of fun and colour. Choose bold jewel colours or work with tonal shades with bold bunting at the hem. As an alternative add the bunting triangles to the hem of a simple A-line dress in rainbow colours.

YOU WILL NEED

- A-line dress and plain collar patterns (following the marked lines for a seamed shoulder)
- Approx. 4 × 60cm (23in) squares of fabric in contrasting colours
- Tailor's chalk
- Approx. 30 × 80cm (12 × 32in) fabric for the facing (optional)
- 1 length of lining fabric (optional) (see Calculating fabric lengths, below)
- 10 rectangles of fabric for the bunting, each 12 × 7cm (5 × 3in)
- Matching sewing threads
- Button

CUTTING OUT

1. Choose the best size for your child, using the guide on page 30. Trace the pattern for the A-line dress in the envelope, following the lines for the correct size. Make a full pattern for the front, with the neck sitting lower, and another full pattern for the back.

2. Divide each pattern into quarters vertically and horizontally across the body, roughly 8cm (3in) below the armholes.

3. Select contrasting colours for each panel. Press the fabric pieces for the dress and lay them out flat. Place the pattern pieces in position on the fabric, making sure the centre front and centre back are parallel to the selvedge.

4. Mark around the pattern pieces using tailor's chalk, adding 1cm (³/₈in) all around but 2cm (³/₄in) at the hem. Carefully cut the pieces out

5. To make the dress with facings around the neck and armholes, simply cut facing by drawing a straight line across the body pattern 4cm (1¹/₂in) below the armholes. The facing may be cut from the main fabric or something lighter in weight, in either a contrast or matching fabric.

6. To make a fully lined dress you will need to cut a complete new dress in lining fabric at least 2cm (³/₄in) shorter in length.

(CON'T)

CALCULATING LINING LENGTHS	6 months–3 years	3–7 years
Width 110cm (44in)	70cm (27¹/₂in)	80cm (31¹/₂in)
Width 150cm (60in)	70cm (27¹/₂in)	80cm (31¹/₂in)

SEWING PANELS

1. Sew the four front panels together, first the lower two panels, then the upper two panels. Then sew both sections together.

2. Sew each upper back panel to the corresponding lower back panel, leaving the entire centre back open.

BUNTING

1. Cut 10 rectangles of fabric in different colours, each 12 × 7 cm (5 × 3in).

2. Fold each rectangle in half lengthways and sew along one edge, 1 cm (³⁄₈in) from the edge.

3. Trim the corner as shown and turn the bunting through.

4. Shape it into a triangle with the seam centre back and press.

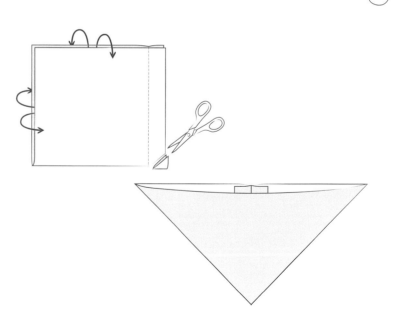

COLLAR AND NECKLINE

1. Cut two collars (the right side and the facing), using the collar pattern on the web (see page 11). The pattern is for the left only, and should be flipped over to make the right collar. It is unlikely you will need to strengthen the collar as it is simply for decoration; however, if you do, press an iron-on interfacing to the reverse of the collar facing.

2. Place the pieces right sides together and sew around the curved outer edges of the collar.

3. Snip into the curves to create a smooth, curved edge when turned back through. Turn through.

4. Press, then topstitch the outer edge 5mm (¼in) from the edge.

5. Place the front and back of the dress right sides together and sew the shoulder seams 1cm (⅜in) from the edge. Press the seams open. Repeat for the facings (or lining).

6. Pin the two prepared collar pieces on to the dress, facing side to the right side of the dress, working from the centre of the neck outwards. Note the collar shape is different at the back than the front, so be sure you are positioning the pieces correctly. Sew into position.

7. Now place the facing (or lining) onto the dress right sides together and sew around the neckline, trapping the collar within. Repeat for the armholes, taking care not to catch the collar into the seam. It may help to roll the collar a little so it doesn't get in the way when you're sewing. Snip into the curves around the neckline and the armholes. Turn the dress through and press.

SEWING SEAMS AND JOINING

1. Overlock all seams and the remaining raw edges.

2. On the main dress, mark the length of your zip or neck opening of 8cm (3in) from the top of the neckline down the back. Sew a seam from the hemline to this point. Press the seam open, continuing to press right to the neck. Repeat for the facing (or lining).

3. Prepare a rouleau loop from the main fabric (see Option A for the Simple A-line dress on page 40). Fold the rouleau to make a loop and pin it in position at the neck opening. The loop should be large enough to comfortably fit around your button. Complete the neck opening by sewing the dress fabric and facing (or lining) 2mm (⅛in) from the edge, all the way around the opening.

4. Pin the side seams, right sides of the dress and rights side of the facing (or lining) together, carefully matching at the armhole seam. Sew and press.

FINISHING

1. Pin the 10 triangles of bunting into place along the hemline. Sew them in place and overlock the edges to finish. Turn the edges back and topstitch so the hemline sits flat.

2. Finish the hem on the facing (or lining) by overlocking the hem edge, turning it back and stitching it down, 1cm (⅜in) from the edge.

3. Topstitch around the arm and neck edges 5mm (¼in) from the edges, taking care around the curves.

4. Sew the button into place.

Funky romper

This sweet romper makes an easy-to-wear shape with adjustable shoulder ties to fit. It's perfect for sunny days – I've cropped it just above the ankle, but can be shortened if you choose. It's a perfect pattern for funky cotton prints, but made in heavier fabrics like cotton corduroy and worn layered, it makes a perfect winter dungaree too. My daughters love this style as it gives them room to move and play.

YOU WILL NEED

- Romper, yoke and pocket patterns
- 75cm (³⁄₄yd) medium-weight printed fabric
- 25cm (10in) or one fat quarter of contrast cotton fabric for the yoke, straps and ties
- Contrast fabric for pockets, if desired
- 1m (1yd) narrow elastic, 1cm (³⁄₈in) wide
- Matching sewing threads
- Tailor's chalk

CUTTING OUT

1. Choose the best size for your child. Trace the pattern for the Romper in the envelope, following the lines for the correct size.

2. Press the main fabric and arrange it on a flat surface so you can cut out a right front/back and a left front/back. Make sure the grain line is parallel to the selvedge and any pattern runs in the right direction.

3. Mark around the pattern pieces using tailor's chalk, adding 1cm (³⁄₈in) all around. Cut the pieces out carefully.

4. Trace the pattern pieces for the yoke, rounded pocket and ankle cuff. Cut four strips of contrast fabric, each measuring 30 × 5cm (12 × 2in). Cut four yokes, two ankle cuffs and two pockets from the contrast fabrics, adding 1cm (³⁄₈in) all around.

YOKE AND TIES

1. To create ties, prepare four strips of fabric, each measuring 30 × 5cm (12 × 2in). Press both long edges and one short edge in 5mm (¹⁄₄in) on all four strips of fabric. Fold each in half lengthways and press again. Stitch around the outer edges.

2. You can also use ribbon as ties but make sure you finish one raw cut end on each ribbon.

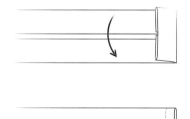

(CON'T)

3. Place two yoke sections right sides together, with one strap positioned at each top corner between the layers. Pin and sew along the sides and top edge, securing the straps in place on the top edge.

4. Snip away the excess at the corners, turn through and press. Repeat for the other yoke.

ANKLE CUFFS AND POCKETS

1. Sew the cuffs to the bottom edge of each romper piece. Overlock the edges.

2. Finish the bottom edge of each cuff with a small rolled hem, by turning back twice by 5mm (¼in) and stitching. Alternatively, overlock, turn back and stitch in place.

3. Now add the elastic to each cuff. Mark a line around the centre and sew a 22cm (9in) length of narrow elastic into place, stretching it gently as you go to create a soft gather. You may require a little more or less elastic, depending on the size you are making. Repeat for the other leg.

4. Make the pockets by overlocking the edges. Fold and press the bottom and side edges under by 5mm (¼in), and the pocket top by 1cm (³⁄₈in). Thread elastic through the pocket top and secure at each end to create a gathered pocket. See page 50 for more detail.

5. Pin the pockets into place on the romper fronts. Topstitch them in place, reinforcing the start and finish with a small triangle.

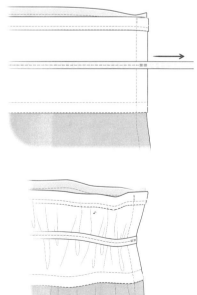

SEWING SEAMS AND JOINING

1. Assemble the romper by placing the pieces right sides together and sewing the centre front and back seams. Overlock and press.

2. Sew the inside leg seams, including the contrast cuff. Overlock and press.

3. Overlock the armhole edges, turn back 5mm (¼in), then stitch. Alternatively, create a rolled finish by turning back 3mm (⅛in), then again and stitching.

4. Gather the back and front top edges of the romper to 19cm (7½in).

5. Pin the yoke front to the front face of the romper right sides together. Sew into place, 1cm (⅜in) from the edge. Press the raw edges into the yoke. Overlock the lower edge of the yoke facing. Repeat for the back yoke.

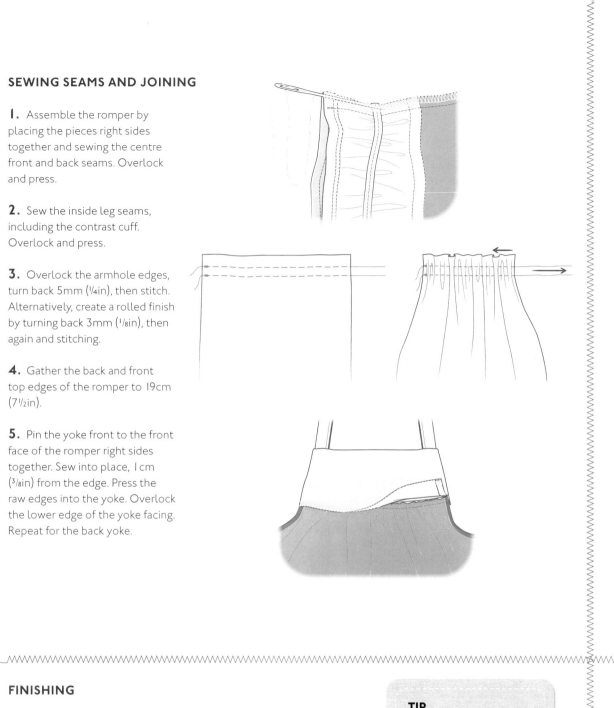

FINISHING

To finish, topstitch around both yokes 5mm (¼in) from the edges.

> **TIP**
> Try contrast pockets and ties, to give the romper a more personal look.

Bumblebee shortie romper

This romper is perfect for hot sunny days on the beach or in the garden, is easy to wear, and is cut above the ankle to show off those beautiful feet. Perfect for little babies, it has a real cute factor. You can also try making it in red, adding black spots instead of stripes to make a lady bird.

YOU WILL NEED

- Romper, face and antenna patterns (following the lines for the short leg without a cuff)
- 75cm (¾yd) of medium-weight yellow fabric
- 25cm (10in) contrast black cotton fabric for the yoke and stripes
- Tailor's chalk
- 1m (1yd) narrow elastic, 1cm (³/₈in) wide
- Matching sewing threads
- Soft wadding or toy filling for the bee antennae (you can use soft fabric scraps if you prefer)
- 2 contrast buttons for the eyes, approx. 2cm (³/₄in) in diameter

CUTTING OUT

1. Choose the best size for your child, using the guide on page 30. Trace the pattern for the Romper in the envelope, following the lines for the correct size and length of leg.

2. Press the main fabric and arrange it on a flat surface so you can cut out a right front/back and a left front/back. Make sure the grain line is parallel to the selvedge and any pattern runs in the right direction.

3. Mark around the pattern pieces using tailor's chalk, adding 1cm (³/₈in) all around. Cut the pieces out carefully.

4. Also from the yellow fabric, cut two front ties measuring 30 × 5cm (12 × 2in) and one back tie measuring 70 × 5cm(28 × 2in).

5. Trace the pattern pieces for the romper face and the antenna. From the black fabric, cut two face panels, four antenna pieces and four strips as long as the width of the romper for stripes, adding 1cm (3/8in) all around.

(CON'T)

ANTENNAE AND STRIPES

1. Place two antennae pieces right sides together and sew around the keyhole shaped edge, leaving the end open. Clip into the curved edges and turn through. Using a pencil, gently fill the antenna with soft wadding or toy filler. Repeat with the second antenna.

2. To prepare the stripes, press the long raw edges in by 1 cm (3/8in). Pin them into position on the two body sections, then sew them into place, taking care to position them accurately so they will match at the centre front and back seams.

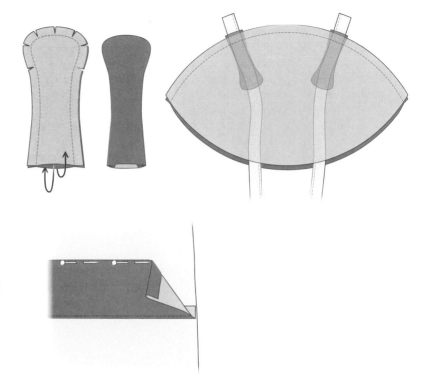

YOKE FACE AND TIES

1. To create the front ties, prepare two strips of fabric measuring 30 × 5cm (12 × 2in). Press both long edges and one short edge inwards by 5mm (1/4in) on both strips of fabric. Fold each in half lengthways and press again. Stitch around the outer edges.

2. To create the longer back ties, prepare two strips of fabric measuring 70 × 5cm (28 × 2in). Press both long edges and one short end inwards by 5mm (1/4in) on both strips of the fabric. Fold in half lengthways and press again. Stitch around the outer edges.

3. Place two yoke sections right sides together. You may wish to back one of the pieces with interfacing or a single layer of fabric to make the yoke more substantial. Pin the yokes together, trapping a strap and antennae between the layers. Stitch around the top edge of the yoke.

4. Clip into the seamed edge, turn through and press.

ELASTICATING THE LEG HEM

1. Finish the bottom edge of each leg with a small rolled hem by turning back twice by 5mm (¼in) and stitching. Alternatively, overlock, turn back and stitch in place.

2. Now add the elastic around each leg. Mark a line around the leg 2.5cm (1in) from the bottom edge. Sew a 22cm (9in) length of narrow elastic along the line, stretching it gently as you go to create a soft gather. You may require a little more or less elastic depending on the size you are making. Repeat for the other leg.

SEWING SEAMS AND JOINING

1. Assemble the romper by placing right sides together and sewing the centre front and back seams. Make sure the stripes are matched centre front and centre back. Overlock.

2. Sew the inside leg seams. Overlock.

3. Overlock the armhole edges, turn back 5mm (¼in), then stitch. Alternatively, create a rolled finish by turning back 3mm (⅛in), then again and stitching.

ADDING THE YOKE AND STRAPS

1. Gather the top edge of the front of the romper to 19cm (7½in).

2. Turn back the top edge of the back of the romper by 1cm (⅜in), then 2cm (¾in) to create a channel for the back tie. Stitch, leaving openings at both ends. Press.

3. Pin the front yoke to the front of the romper, right sides together. Sew into place, 1cm (⅜in) from the edge. Press the raw edges into the yoke. Overlock the lower edge of the yoke facing.

4. To finish, press, then topstitch around the yoke, 5mm (¼in) from the edges.

FINISHING

1. Use a safety pin to thread the long strap through the back channel, then gather to the desired fit.

2. Sew the button eyes into place on the yolk.

Seaside sundress

This simple pillowcase dress shape is perfect for lazy, hazy summer days. Ideal for beginners, it's easy to make, either plain, in a funky print, or as here, with a seaside appliqué. Very retro and, for me, a reminder of childhood beach holidays and growing up by the sea.

YOU WILL NEED

- A-line dress pattern (follow the lines for the sundress)
- 75cm (30in) medium- to lightweight pale blue plain fabric
- Tailor's chalk
- 10 × 100cm (4 × 40in) mid-blue fabric for the water
- 10 × 100cm (4 × 40in) dark blue fabric or jumbo ric rac for the waves
- 75 × 10cm (30 × 4in) fabric for the straps
- Iron-on, double-sided adhesive web
- 15cm (6in) square yellow fabric or felt for the sun
- Contrast plain or patterned fabric for the boat
- Matching sewing threads

TIP
The straps can be made from self-fabric, however you can use 2cm (³⁄₄in) wide ribbon instead.

CUTTING OUT

1. Choose the best size for your child, using the guide on page 30. Trace the pattern for the A-line dress in the envelope, following the lines for the sundress and the correct size.

2. Press the main fabric and arrange it on a flat surface so you can cut out a whole front and a whole back. Make sure the grain lines on the pattern are parallel to the selvedge.

3. Mark around the pattern pieces using tailor's chalk, adding 1cm (³⁄₈in) all around. Cut the pieces out carefully.

(CON'T)

APPLIQUÉ

1. Sew one side seam and finish by overlocking. Press, and open the dress out flat.

2. Pin the strip of mid-blue fabric to the bottom edge of the dress, right sides together. Trim any excess at the sides. Sew together, with a 1cm (³/8in) seam allowance. Press the seam open.

3. To add the waves you can use jumbo ric rac. Alternatively, use the template (see page 199) to cut them from dark blue fabric. Back the waves with adhesive web and, if peeling off the backing paper, position the waves over the edge of the blue water panel. Stitch the waves into place along the top and bottom to secure.

4. Cut the sun from yellow fabric or felt using the template on page 199. Bond the sun in position on the front of the dress using adhesive web.

5. Repeat for the little boat. You can try favourite colours or printed fabrics here.

6. Sew around all raw edges, close to the edge.

SEWING SEAMS AND JOINING

1. Overlock the raw edges on the sides, armholes and top edges.

2. Sew the side seam and press open.

3. Turn back the armhole edges by 5mm (¼in) and sew. Press.

4. Turn back the top edge of the dress by 2.5cm (1in) to create a channel for the ties. Stitch, leaving openings at both ends. Press.

5. Turn a double hem on the bottom edge of the dress and stitch in place.

STRAPS

1. Cut two straps of plain fabric, each measuring 75 × 5cm (30 × 2in). Fold both long edges and one short edge in by 5mm (¼in) on both pieces. Fold each in half lengthwise, press, then stitch along the open edge and ends to secure. Press.

2. If you want to use ribbon, simply cut to length and hand finish the raw ends by rolling them back and stitching them into place.

3. Insert one strap through each channel with a large safety pin or paper clip and gather the top edges to fit.

Baby bunting sundress

This set is perfect for hot summer days in the garden; it's lovely and cool and will show off those gorgeous legs. Add colour with a spectrum of bunting, or choose some vintage or special fabrics to create little dresses on a washing line. To create a pair of matching knickers, see page 118.

YOU WILL NEED

- A-line dress and yoke patterns (follow the lines for the sundress)
- Bunting template
- 75cm (30in) medium-weight printed fabric
- Tailor's chalk
- 25cm (10in) or one fat quarter of contrast cotton fabric for the yoke and ties
- Iron-on, double-sided adhesive web
- Assorted small pieces of coloured scraps for the bunting flags
- Matching sewing threads
- 1m (1yd) narrow elastic for the knicker edges

CUTTING OUT

1. Choose the best size for your child, using the guide on page 30. Trace the pattern for the A-line dress in the envelope, following the lines for the sundress and the correct size.

2. Press the main fabric and arrange it on a flat surface so you can cut out a whole front and a whole back. Make sure the grain lines on the pattern are parallel to the selvedge.

3. Mark around the pattern pieces using tailor's chalk, adding 1cm ($^3/_8$in) all around. Cut the pieces out carefully.

4. Trace the pattern piece for the yoke and cut out four yokes from the contrast fabric. Cut four strips of contrast fabric, each measuring 30 × 5cm (12 × 2in), for the straps.

ADDING DETAIL

1. Sew one side seam and finish by overlocking. Press and open the dress out flat.

(CON'T)

2. For the bunting line, back enough fabric with adhesive web to cut several 5mm (¼in) wide strips, approximately 75cm (30in) in length. Alternatively, you may use narrow ribbon. Draw a chalk line where you would like the bunting to wrap around the dress front to back. Make sure the line starts and finishes when the sides are joined, so it runs right around the dress. Pin the strip in place, stitch and press.

3. Cut a range of lovely bright triangles for the bunting, using the template on page 200. Back the shapes with adhesive web. Then, peeling off the backing paper, press the bunting into place along the line. Sew around all the edges with matching thread close to the edge.

SEWING SEAMS AND JOINING

1. Sew the remaining side seam and overlock to finish.

2. Turn back the hem edge by 1cm (³⁄₈in), then another 1cm (³⁄₈in), press and stitch.

3. Overlock the armhole edges, turning back by 5mm (¼in), then stitch.

4. Gather the top edge of the front and back dress to 19cm (7½in) (see page 24).

YOKE AND TIES

1. To create ties, prepare four strips of fabric, each measuring 30 × 5cm (12 × 2in). Press both long edges and one short edge in 5mm (¼in) on all four strips of fabric. Fold each in half lengthways and press again. Stitch around the outer edges.

2. Place two yoke sections right sides together, with one strap positioned at each top corner between the layers. Pin and sew along the sides and top edge, securing the straps in place on the top edge.

3. Snip away the excess at the corners, turn through and press.

4. Pin the front yoke to the dress front, right sides together. Sew it into place, 1cm (³⁄₈in) from the edge. Press the raw edges into the yoke. Overlock the lower edge of the yoke facing.

EASY ALTERNATIVE

Instead of making a yoke, you could make a simple 'pillowcase' dress top by following instructions for the top of the seaside sundress (see page 84).

This is a simple option, but remember to add 3cm, (1¼in) to the top edges to create channels for the ties.

FINISHING

Topstitch around the yoke, 5mm (¼in) from the edges.

Baby sun set

This little dress set is perfect for hot sunny days on the beach and people-watching from the pram. Make it with matching knickers or bloomers (see pages 118 and 120), or on its own as a super-easy project. The top is elasticated, creating a soft pillowcase edge, which stays in place when worn.

YOU WILL NEED

- A-line dress pattern (follow the lines for the sundress)
- 75cm (30in) medium-weight printed fabric
- Tailor's chalk
- 25cm (10in) or one fat quarter of fabric for the straps and pockets
- Matching sewing threads
- 1.5m (1½ yd) narrow elastic for pockets

CUTTING OUT

1. Choose the best size for your child, using the guide on page 30. Trace the pattern for the A-line dress in the envelope, following the lines for the sundress and the correct size.

2. Press the main fabric and arrange it on a flat surface so you can cut out a whole front and a whole back. Make sure the grain lines on the pattern are parallel to the selvedge.

3. Mark around the pattern pieces using tailor's chalk, adding 1cm (³⁄₈in) all around. Cut the pieces out carefully.

(CON'T)

STRAPS AND POCKETS

1. Cut four strips of contrast fabric, each measuring 30 × 5cm (12 × 2in). Press both long edges and one short edge in by 5mm (¼in) on each strip. Fold each in half lengthways and press again. Stitch around the outer edges to create the straps. To make things easier, you can use ribbon as ties but finish the cut ends first.

2. Cut two pockets from contrast fabric. Overlock the edges. Fold and press the side and bottom edges under by 5mm (¼in), and the pocket top by 1cm (⅜in). Thread the elastic through the channel and secure it at each end to create a gathered pocket. Simple patch pockets can be added for ease if you prefer. See the Rainbow dress pocket on page 50 for more detail.

3. Pin the pockets into place on the dress front. Sew down, reinforcing with a small triangle at the start and finish.

4. Sew the side seams and overlock to finish. Press

FINISHING

1. Overlock the armhole and top edges.

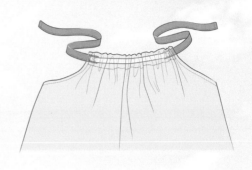

2. Turn back 5mm (¼in) under the arms only and stitch. Alternatively, try a rolled finish by turning back 3mm (⅛in), then again and stitching.

3. Cut two lengths of elastic to 14cm (5½in), or as long as necessary. Sew a strap to each end of both lengths of elastic.

4. Fold the top edge of the front and back of the dress down by 2cm (¾in) and stitch down. Insert one strap through with a large safety pin, until the elastic is encased. Gather the top edge of the dress and secure through the strap at each side. Repeat for the back. This allows you to create a soft elasticated pillowcase shape that stays in place.

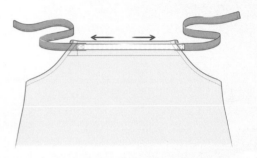

5. Hem the dress by turning under by 1cm (⅜in) twice and sew in place.

Little house apron dress

This dress has a clever twist at the back. It's a simple shape, with room in the large front pockets to stash all manner of things when out and about. Try different colour combinations and shapes to create a gingerbread house or a townhouse. You can draw out a simple house shape to resemble your own sweet abode. The cross-over straps at the back have a charming nostalgic look, while making the dress easy to fit. Wear layered with a jersey tee shirt or simply on its own as a stunning sundress.

YOU WILL NEED

- Apron dress and patterns
- 1m (1yd) medium-weight plain fabric, such as denim, corduroy, linen or canvas
- Tailor's chalk
- 20 × 17cm (8 × 7in) fabric for the pocket
- Contrast plain or patterned fabrics for the windows, door and roof
- Iron-on, double-sided adhesive web
- Approx. 30cm (12in) elastic, 2cm (¾in) wide
- Matching or contrast sewing threads
- 20cm (8in) cotton tape, 1cm (³⁄₈in) wide (you can make this from self fabric)

CUTTING OUT

1. Choose the best size for your child, using the guide on page 30. Trace the patterns for the Apron dress, bib facing and accompanying patch pocket in the envelope, following the lines for the correct size and the lower back.

2. Press the main fabric and arrange it on a flat surface so you can cut out one whole front and one whole back. Make sure the centre front and centre back are parallel to the selvedge.

3. Mark around the pattern pieces using tailor's chalk, adding 1cm (³⁄₈in) all around, but 3cm (1¼in) at the hem and back of waist. Cut the pieces out carefully.

4. Cut two strips of fabric each 85cm (33in) in length, 7cm (3in) wide for the straps.

(CON'T)

POCKET

1. Select fabrics for the roof, windows and door appliqué pieces and bond adhesive web to the reverse. Cut to size using the pattern for the roof, and by cutting simple squares and rectangles to create your own windows and door.

2. Cut out the main pocket. Overlock the edges.

3. Arrange the door and window appliqué pieces in position on the pocket, leaving a generous turn back of approximately 2.5cm (1in) where the pocket opens. Cover with a cloth and press in place.

4. Stitch around the bottom and side edges using matching or contrast thread to secure.

5. Turn back the top edge of the pocket by 2.5cm (1in) and stitch it down. Press under the remaining edges by 1cm (³/₈in).

6. Place the pocket in position on the front of the dress. Pin and stitch it down 2mm (¹/₈in) from the edges, making sure the top of the pocket is secured with a backstitch.

7. Bond the roof in the same way and sew around the edges.

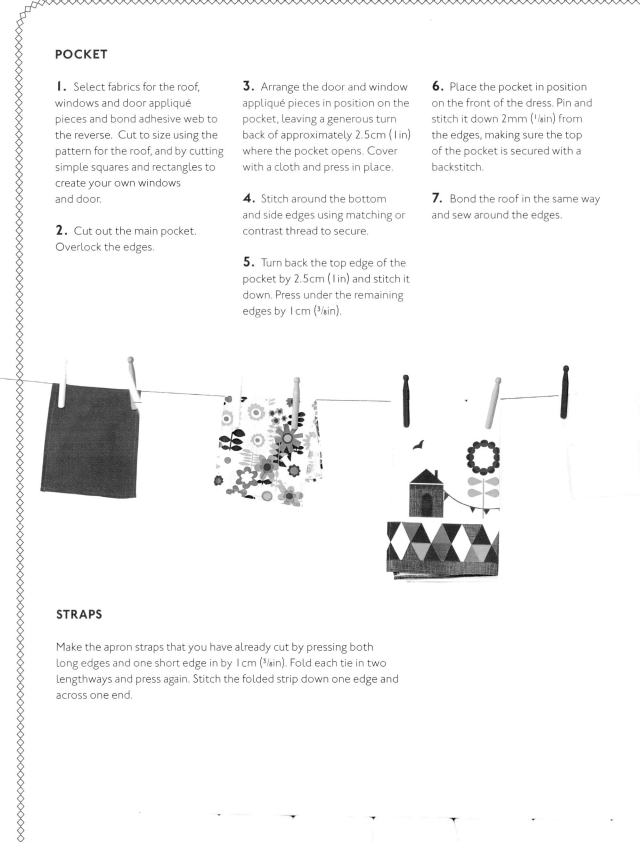

STRAPS

Make the apron straps that you have already cut by pressing both long edges and one short edge in by 1cm (³/₈in). Fold each tie in two lengthways and press again. Stitch the folded strip down one edge and across one end.

SEWING SEAMS AND JOINING

1. Take the back dress piece and turn back the top edge by 1cm (³/₈in). Press, then turn back a further 2.5cm (1in). Stitch it into place.

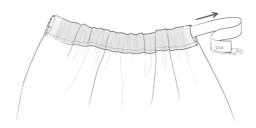

2. Attach a large safety pin to one end of the elastic and feed it through the channel you have created. Smooth out the gathers and secure the elastic at each end by stitching through all the layers to secure it. Estimate how much elastic to use as follows: sizes 6m–2years (20cm/8in), sizes 3–4yrs (23cm/9in), sizes 5–6yrs (25cm/10in).

3. Now assemble the dress by placing the dress front and back right sides together. Sew both side seams and overlock the edges as required.

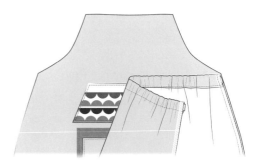

4. Attach one strap to each top corner of the dress bib.

5. Cut the tape into 2 × 10cm (4in) lengths. Fold each in half to form a loop and sew into place on the front bib as marked on the pattern.

6. Lay the bib facing on the dress front right sides together, pin, then sew around the edge. If you're using a heavy fabric, you may need to snip away the corners at right angles, to reduce inside bulk to the corners when turned through. Turn back and press.

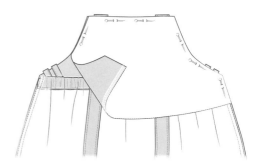

7. Overlock the lower edge of the bib facing.

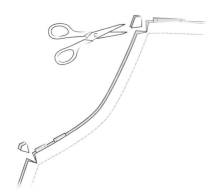

FINISHING

1. Topstitch around the bib 5mm (¹/₄in) from the edge.

2. Hem the dress by turning back twice.

3. Secure the facing inside by slip stitching into place.

4. To wear, the shoulder straps cross at the back, go through the loops and then wrap in a bow to secure.

Little helper apron

This is a super-simple little apron, perfect for beginners, which looks lovely hanging on the back of a door. Your little helper will love having their own special outfit to help grown-ups with jobs around the home. You can use your favourite prints, add simple appliqué shapes, and create a useful pocket for little tools for the kitchen and garden.

YOU WILL NEED

- Apron pattern
- 50 × 60cm (20 × 24in) heavyweight fabric (furnishing fabrics, canvas and oilcloth all work well)
- Tailor's chalk
- 1.5m (1¾yd) cotton webbing tape, 3cm (1¼in) wide
- Fabric for the pocket and appliqué
- Decorative trims (optional)
- Matching sewing threads
- Iron-on, double-sided adhesive web for appliqué

TIPS

Make the apron with a patch or a giant tool pocket. They also look great with scaled down kitchen utensils and garden tool motifs.

Try combinations using some of the templates provided at the back of the book, like the rainbow or cloud motifs. You can scale them up to adult size too.

CUTTING OUT

1. The apron pattern is one size, and fits a child between 1–4 years comfortably. Trace the pattern provided on the web (see page 11). Either make a full pattern or work with half a pattern, placing the centre line on a folded edge. Adjust the length if your child is older or taller.

2. Press the fabric and lay it on a flat surface. Cut the apron piece and pocket from your fabric, adding 1cm (³⁄₈in) all around, but 2cm (¾in) to the top of the pocket.

3. Cut three strips of cotton webbing, each 50cm (20in) long for the ties and neck strap.

POCKET AND TIES

1. Prepare the pocket by turning back the top edge by 1cm (³⁄₈in) twice and sewing.

2. Turn under one end of each tie twice and stitch to secure. Press.

(CON'T)

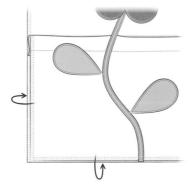
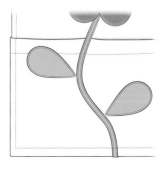

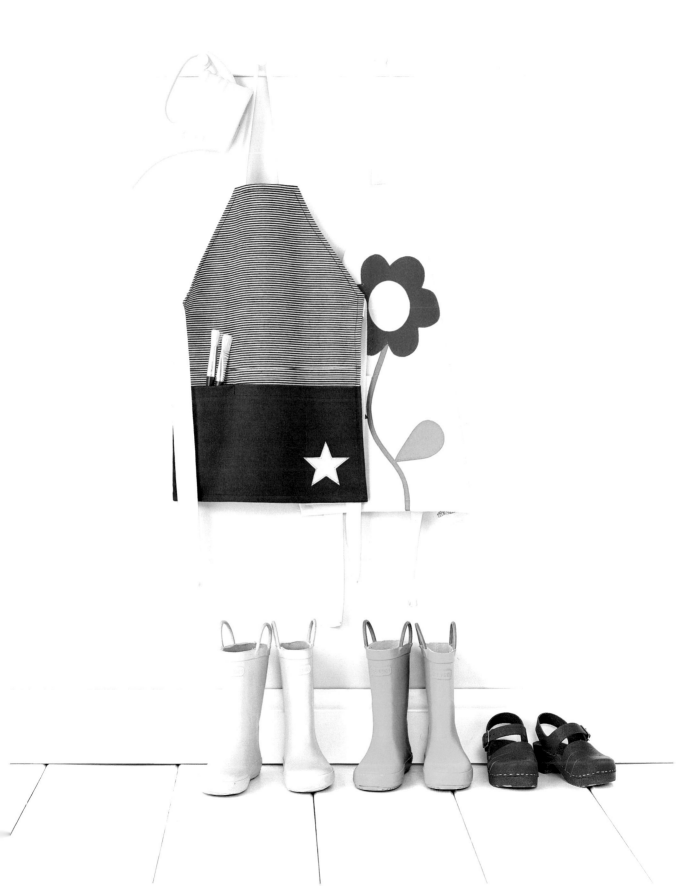

OPTION A
FLOWER APRON

1. Using the flower template on page 197, cut out the flower and leaf shapes, and a wavy strip 1cm (3/8in) wide for the stem from bonded fabric.

2. Place the pocket on the apron. Bond the appliqué shapes to adhesive web. Mark the stem, which will grow from the hem upwards on the pocket. Bond and sew the leaves only into place, keeping the pocket separate.

3. Sew the pocket to the apron around the outer edges. Press. Bond and sew the stem into place up the front and onto the apron. Bond and sew the flower, topstitching into place using matching thread, 2mm (1/8in) from the edges. Press.

OPTION B
STAR APRON

1. Using the star template (page 208) cut out the star shape and bond adhesive web to the fabric shape. Remove the paper backing and applique the shape into place on the pocket, stitching to secure 2mm (1/8in) from the edges.

2. Press the remaining edges to the wrong side. Then position the pocket on the apron and sew it into place, making sure you backstitch the start and finish to secure. Press.

FINISHING

1. Position the waist ties and neck strap into place and sew down.

2. You now need to finish the edges of the apron. The easiest way to do this is to overlock or use a zigzag stitch to prevent from fraying. If using oilcloth or a coated fabric, overlocking is not required.

3. Turn back all the edges by 1cm (3/8in) and sew down, using a backstitch over the tie areas to make these extra secure.

4. Press the edges.

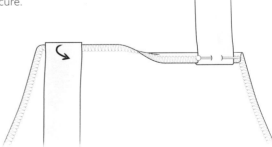

Little painter artist smock ...OR SUN IS UP SWEATER DRESS

This long-sleeved dress pattern is perfect for all manner of fabrics, from woven cotton prints, linen, chambray and corduroy for summer or winter. It also works well in jersey or sweatshirt fabric as a snugly sweater dress. The blue dress opposite is made in denim, with two generous tool pockets to create a comfortable and quite grown-up utility style dress. The grey sunshine dress is made in classic grey marl sweatshirt fabric, with a happy sunshine appliqué added above a generous pouch pocket. If you use jersey, it's a good idea to set your machine stitch to a stretch setting to allow for stretch of the fabric. The pattern is panelled, making it ideal for colour blocking. The dress pattern can be cropped above the pocket line and made into a simple top too.

YOU WILL NEED

- Smock dress, sleeve and pocket patterns
- 1.5m (1¾yd) dress fabric
- Tailor's chalk
- Contrast print or plain fabric for pockets and/or appliqué
- Matching sewing threads
- Iron-on, double-sided adhesive bonding web for appliqué
- 50cm (20in) elastic, 1cm (³⁄₈in) wide

CUTTING OUT

1. Choose the best size for your child, using the guide on page 30. Trace the patterns for the Smock dress and the Smock sleeve on the web (see page 11), following the lines for the correct size. Make a pattern for the front, with the neck sitting lower at the front, and another for the back.

2. Press the fabric and arrange it on a flat surface so you can cut out the smock front and back and two smock sleeves. Make sure the grain lines on the pattern are parallel to the selvedge. You can choose whether to make the front and back as one piece each or whether to make an upper and lower panel for each.

3. Mark around the pattern pieces using tailor's chalk, adding 1cm (³⁄₈in) all around, but 2cm (¾ in) at the hem. Cut the pieces out carefully, still on a flat surface.

4. Cut out either one or two pockets in the main or contrast fabric.

5. Cut one bias strip of main fabric, 60 × 4cm (24 × 1½in) for the neck facing.

(CON'T)

POCKET

1. If you have chosen to make the painter smock in panels, first assemble the front upper and lower panels, and the back upper and lower panels, by sewing right sides together. Overlock and press.

2. Prepare the pocket(s) by overlocking all the edges. Turn back the top edge by 1 cm (³/₈in), then 2 cm (³/₄in) and sew. I have made a contrast pocket top by adding binding to finish (see page 19). If you are making one pocket, press the remaining edges to the wrong side. If you are making two pockets, press the bottom and one side edge on each pocket to the wrong side. Position the two pockets on each side of the front smock, so that the outer edges will be sewn into the seams.

3. If you are adding the sunshine appliqué, trace the template on page 201. Prepare a piece of yellow cotton fabric by backing it with iron-on adhesive web, following the manufacturer's instructions. Prepare bonded fabrics for the eyes, cheeks and mouth. Trace off and cut out the appliqué shapes. Peel the paper backing away, and place the design in place on the lower edge of the front top panel. Press it in place, then stitch all around to secure it, using matching sewing thread.

4. Sew the pocket(s) in place, making sure you backstitch or reinforce the start and finish to secure.

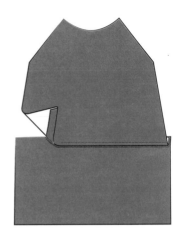

(CON'T)

SEWING SEAMS AND JOINING

1. Assemble the front and back to the raglan sleeves, overlock and press. You will now have a continuous neckline.

2. Measure the exact length of bias facing needed to extend around the neckline, plus 2 cm (¾in) seam allowance, and cut to size. Sew the two short ends right sides together to create a continuous piece.

3. With right sides together and positioning the facing seam at the back, sew the facing around the neckline, pinning first if you wish so the facing sits evenly. Press the facing back. Now turn the facing through to the inside of the smock and pin it into place to the inside of the neckline.

4. Turning the raw edge of the facing under, carefully sew it in place, leaving a small gap of 2 cm (¾in) to create an opening. Using a safety pin, thread elastic into the neckline. Gather the neckline to fit, stitch to secure the ends of the elastic, then sew the opening closed.

5. Position the front and back, right sides together, matching the side seams. Sew the side seams along the smock and underarms. Overlock and press.

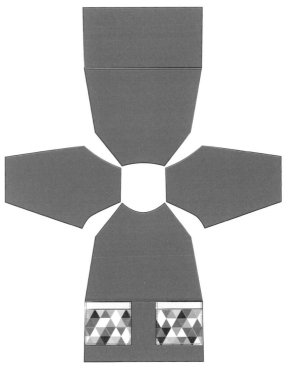

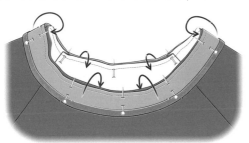

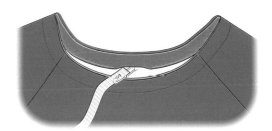

FINISHING

Finally, hem the bottom of the sleeves and the smock hem by turning back once by 1 cm (⅜in), then by 2 cm (¾in) and sewing down. If you are using stretch fabric, overlock the edges first and turn back once by 2.5 cm (1 in), then sew down. Press.

TIP

For the painter smock, I have created a contrast facing. You can see this on the outside of the dress by sewing the bias facing to the inside neck edge first, then folding it out to the front of the dress before sewing it into place.

To gauge the length of elastic needed, place the elastic with a little stretch around your child's head. If you don't have her at hand to measure, you can use the following guide:

6–12 months / 1–2 years	38cm (15in)
2–3 years / 3–4 years	42cm (17in)
4–5 years / 5–6 years / 6–7 years	46cm (18in)

2

Bottoms

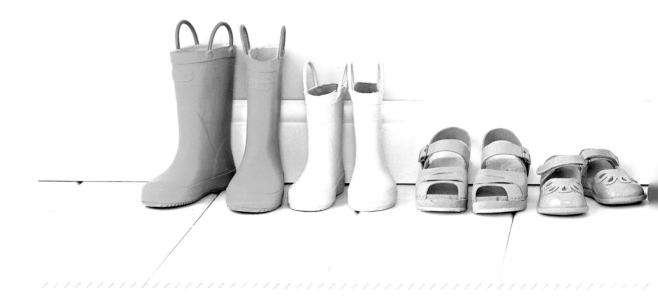

Windy day kite skirt

This delightful pull-on gathered skirt has a 360-degree appliqué. Its simple shape means that it requires no pattern. This skirt can be made using light- or medium-weight fabric.

YOU WILL NEED

- 50cm (20in) fabric, 110cm (44in) or 150cm (60in) wide
- Tailor's chalk
- Kite template
- Narrow ribbon or tape for the kite string
- Coloured fabrics for the kite
- Coloured ribbons for the kite bows
- Iron-on, double-sided adhesive bonding web
- 60cm (24in) elastic, 2cm (¾in) wide
- Matching sewing threads

CUTTING OUT

1. First measure your child's waist and cut the elastic to size, deducting 5cm (2in). Decide how long you want the skirt and add 4cm (1½in) for the hem and waistband. Cut your fabric to this measurement across the fabric, so the grain runs vertically down the skirt.

2. Bond adhesive web to the kite fabrics and, using the template on page 202, cut out four triangles.

ADDING DETAIL

1. Mark the position of the kite at one end of the skirt length. Then draw a freehand line across the skirt to mark the position of the kite tail, making a loop as you go.

2. Take the narrow tape or ribbon and stitch this on to the drawn line to make the kite string.

3. Peeling off the paper backing, position the kite triangles into place, and bond them to the skirt, pressing with an iron. Stitch around the edges of the kite close to the edges to secure.

4. Add little bows along the length of the kite tail in bright coloured ribbon. These can be made by cutting ribbon approximately 15cm (6in) in length, folding and sewing down, adding a small tuck as you sew.

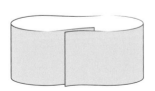

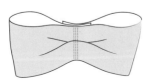

(CON'T)

JOINING THE SKIRT

1. Overlock all the edges of the skirt fabric.

2. Press back the hem by 2cm (¾in) and the waist channel by 2cm (¾in), leaving an opening at the waist through which to thread the elastic.

3. Then sew the side seam to create a tube of fabric.

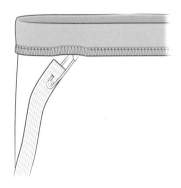

4. Sew the hem and waist channel.

5. Fix a large safety pin to one end of the elastic and thread it through the channel, making sure you secure the opposite end of the elastic. Sew the two ends of the elastic together to secure. Then sew closed the channel opening.

6. Arrange the fabric so that it sits evenly along the elastic, then carefully sew through all the layers at the left and right sides of the waist to secure the elastic and prevent it from rolling.

Carousel skirt

This simple, vibrant skirt is perfect for little girls who love to dance and twirl. I've used simple colour blocks, but it works well with patched fabrics too. It requires a single simple pattern piece, and working with fat quarters means you can choose some lovely printed cotton quilter's fabrics sold by the fat quarter.

YOU WILL NEED

- Four fat quarter fabrics, four 50cm (20in) square pieces, or assorted pieces measuring 23 × 13cm (9 × 5¼in)
- Tailor's chalk
- Matching fabric for the waistband
- Elastic for the waistband, 1.5cm (⅝in) wide
- Matching sewing threads

CUTTING OUT AND SEWING SEAMS

1. Choose the best size for your child, using the guide on page 30. Trace the pattern for the Carousel skirt in the envelope, following the lines for the correct size.

2. Select contrasting colours for each of the eight panels. I've chosen four fabrics, to give two panels of each colour.

3. Press the fabric pieces for the skirt and lay them flat. Place the pattern in position on the fabric.

4. Mark around the pattern using tailor's chalk, adding 1cm (⅜in) at the sides and edges, 2cm (¾in) at the hem and 5cm (2in) at the waist.

5. Sew all the panels together, down the sides, in the sequence desired. Overlock all the edges.

(CON'T)

TIP
This skirt is a perfect way to upcycle any treasured offcuts or vintage keepsakes. The hem can be bordered with either bunting or a scalloped edge, turning this simple skirt into a bold statement.

SCALLOPS

1. You will need 16 semicircles of fabric. The finished diameters will be as follows, but add 1 cm (³/₈in) all around:

6 months–2 years   14 (5in)
3–5 years   16 (6in)
5–8 years   18 (7in)

2. For each scallop, place two semicircles together and sew around the curved edge, 1 cm (³/₈in) from the edge.

3. Snip into the seam allowance as shown and turn the scallop through. Press.

4. Repeat to make eight scallops.

TIP
Instead of scallops, try creating a bunting hem as an alternative. Cut eight rectangles of either 14 × 7 cm (5½ × 3¾in), 16 × 8 cm (6¼ × 3¼in), or 18 × 9 cm (7 × 3½in), depending on the skirt size. Fold each rectangle of fabric in half lengthways and sew along one edge, 2 cm (³/₈in) from the edge. Trim the folded corner (see page 74) and turn through. Shape into a triangle with the seam centre back and press.

FINISHING

1. Pin the scallops in place along the hemline, matching them to the side seams on the skirt. Sew them in place and overlock the edges to finish. Turn back, press, and topstitch so that the hemline sits flat.

2. You may wish to add a row of tape 2 cm (¾in) deep to cover the edges of the scallops on the inside.

3. Overlock the waist edge and turn back by 2 cm (¾in). Sew the folded edge down to create a channel into which you can insert the elastic, leaving a gap of approximately 3 cm (1¼in).

4. Measure your child's waist and deduct 3 cm (1¼in) to give the required length of elastic.

5. Insert the elastic with a large safety pin, securing the end as you go so that it doesn't disappear into the channel. When you have threaded all the way through, arrange the elastic so that it isn't twisted, and sew the ends together securely, back and forth.

6. Now sew the opening closed. Arrange the gathers to sit evenly.

Baby knickers

These little knickers are perfect for the beach or worn with shorter summer dresses. They really give a nostalgic feel to an outfit. The pattern is sized up to age 3–4 years, and makes a perfect nappy cover. Adding gathered ruffles to the back section makes a lovely finish for babies taking their first steps.

YOU WILL NEED

- Knicker pattern
- 25cm (10in) or one fat quarter of fabric
- Tailor's chalk
- 1m (1yd) narrow elastic, 5mm (¼in) wide
- Matching sewing threads

CUTTING OUT

1. Choose the best size for your child, using the guide below. Trace the pattern for the Knickers on the web (see page 11), following the lines for the correct size.

2. Press the fabric and lay it on a flat surface, right side up. Mark the pattern on the fabric and cut out, adding 1cm (³⁄8in) seam allowance all around.

SEWING SEAMS AND JOINING

1. Overlock all the edges. Sew the gusset seam and side seams, placing right sides together. Make sure you backstitch at the start and end of each seam to secure.

2. Cut one length of waist and two lengths of leg elastic to size, referring to the chart below. Adjust according to your child's size. Sew the ends of each length of elastic together to form circular pieces.

ADDING THE ELASTIC

Sew the elastic in place into the leg openings and waist of the knickers in turn, creating a narrow channel as you go.

CALCULATING FABRIC SIZES	Waist	Leg
6-18 months	44cm (17¼in)	27cm (10¼in)
18 months-3 years	48cm (19in)	30cm (12in)

Bloomers

These bloomers are gorgeous worn as an extra layer under A-line dresses. The shape is the same as the romper, cut just above the waist, making the romper pattern a really versatile, easy-to-wear shape.

YOU WILL NEED

- Romper pattern (follow the line marked above the waist)
- 50cm (20in) or two fat quarters of medium-weight printed fabric
- Tailor's chalk
- 1m (1yd) narrow elastic, 1cm (3/8in) wide
- Matching sewing threads

CUTTING OUT

1. Choose the best size for your child. Trace the pattern for the Romper in the envelope, following the lines for the correct size and cutting along the bloomer line.

2. Press the fabric and, laying it on a flat surface so you can cut out a right front/back and a left front/back. Make sure the grain line is parallel to the selvedge. Mark the cuff line. Carefully cut around the pattern, adding 1cm (3/8in) all around, to give you a right front/back and a left front/back.

(CON'T)

SEWING SEAMS AND JOINING

1. Finish the bottom edge of each leg with a small rolled hem by turning back twice by 5mm (¼in) and stitching. Press.

2. Now elasticate the hem. Mark a line around the centre line of the cuff and sew a 22cm (8½in) length of narrow elastic into place, stretching it gently as you go to create a soft gather. For smaller sizes you may need a little less elastic to create the gather. Repeat for the other leg.

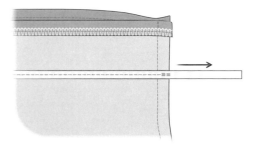

3. Assemble the bloomers by placing the pieces right sides together and sewing the centre front and back seams. Overlock and press.

4. Sew the inside leg seams. Overlock and press.

5. Overlock the top waist edge. Create a waist channel of 1.5cm (⅝in), leaving an opening to insert the elastic.

6. Measure your child's waist (or see the guide on page 30), deduct 5cm (2in) from this measurement and cut elastic to size.

7. Fix a large safety pin to one end of the elastic and thread it through the channel, making sure you secure the opposite end of the elastic. Sew the two ends of elastic together to secure. Then sew the remaining opening to the channel closed.

8. Arrange the fabric so that it sits evenly along the elastic and is not twisted.

Reversible pull-ons

These trousers are perfect for every day, made using two layers of fabric, and with a cute little bottom patch for cheeky toddlers on the move. Being reversible makes them sturdy and warm, and offers a quick change if the need arises. Try fabrics that are designed to co-ordinate, a print and a plain, or something really soft and warm for the winter months. Adding knee patches would make them extra hard wearing. I've added appliqué fabric triangles around the seat patch to create a sunshine and a little boat to the leg hem. Try adding ears and eyes to the seat patch for a really cute toddler trouser.

YOU WILL NEED

- Dungarees pattern
- 2 × 75cm (30in) length of fabric, or 50cm (20in) for sizes 6 months and 1 year
- Tailor's chalk
- 60cm (24in) elastic, 2cm (³⁄₄in) wide
- Matching or contrasting sewing threads

CUTTING OUT

1. Choose the best size for your child, using the guide below. Trace the pattern for the Dungarees in the envelope, following the lines for the correct size and cutting along the trouser line.

2. Press both pieces of fabric and, laying them on a flat surface, fold them double, right sides together. You could place them on top of each other to cut both trousers out together, carefully aligning the folds. Place the pattern on the fabric, making sure the grain line is parallel to the selvedge. Carefully cut around the pattern, adding 1cm (³⁄₈in) all around, to give you two right front/backs and two left front/backs.

(CON'T)

SIZE GUIDE

Age	Height
6–18 months	to 80cm (31½in)
18 months–3 years	to 98cm (39in)
3–5 years	to 110cm (43in)

WILD THINGS

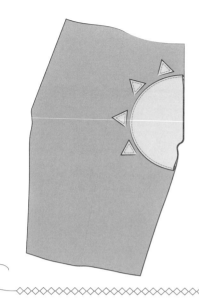

ADDING THE BOTTOM PATCH

Cut two bottom patch panels from contrast fabric, using the shape on the Dungaree pattern. Turn back the curved edges and press. Pin the panels into place on the dungarees as marked on the pattern, then topstitch down. Adding the bottom patch makes a lovely detail, especially for little crawlers, and also adds a layer of durability to the trousers. Appliqué triangles of contrast fabric around the shapes to make the sun.

SEWING SEAMS AND JOINING

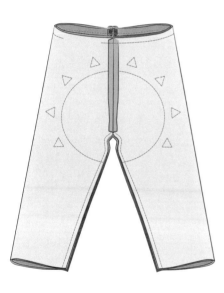

1. Place two matching trouser panels right sides together and sew the centre front and centre back seams with a 1cm (³/₈in) seam allowance. It's worth stitching the back seam twice to make it extra hard-wearing. Overlock the edges and press the seam back. Repeat for the second trousers.

2. Sew the inside leg seams on both pairs of trousers.

3. Now turn one pair of trousers through and layer right sides facing.

4. Sew the two pairs of trousers together around the waistline.

5. Turn the trousers through to the right sides, through one of the legs, and press to give a neat finish at the waist.

6. Sew the waist channel 2.5cm (1in) from the top edge, leaving an opening for the elastic.

7. Now measure your child's waist (or see the guide on page 30) and deduct 5cm (2in) from this measurement to give the elastic length.

8. Thread the elastic through the channel with a large safety pin. Sew the ends of the elastic, then the opening closed.

9. It's a good idea to arrange the gathers, then backstitch the sides several times to stop the elastic from rolling.

10. Pin the bottom hems under to match and then sew the hems on each leg together, 5mm (¹/₄in) from the edge.

3
Character
Outfits

Fox dress

This striking little fox dress is perfect for woodland adventures. Made here from a strong orange colour with a contrast white face, you can also try it in a grey fabric to create a lovely arctic fox. This Wild Things classic design is made using a generic character dress pattern, making it easy to switch with faces from other projects.

YOU WILL NEED

- Character dress patterns: front, back, yoke, strap and pocket
- Fox face template
- 1 length of soft medium-weight, orange woven cotton fabric, such as corduroy, velvet, or cotton twill (see Calculating fabric lengths, below)
- Tailor's chalk
- Cotton fabric scraps in cream, patterned, and brown
- White felt scraps
- 30cm (12in) square of iron-on, double-sided adhesive web
- Matching sewing threads
- 2 or 4 buttons

CUTTING OUT

1. Choose the best size for your child, using the guide on page 30. Trace the patterns for the Character dress in the envelope, following the lines for the correct size and the side extensions for the dress back.

2. Press the main fabric and arrange it on a flat surface so that you can cut out one front, one back, one facing, two face bibs and four straps. Make sure the grain lines on the pattern are parallel to the selvedge and that any pile is running in the right direction.

3. Mark around the pattern pieces using tailor's chalk, adding 1cm (³/₈in) all around, but 2cm (³/₄ in) at the hem. Cut the pieces out carefully.

4. Cut out two pockets from the main fabric or a contrasting fabric.

5. If the yoke needs a little extra weight, cut another bib from plain cotton or interfacing.

6. Using the fox face template on page 203, cut out the left and right face panels from the cream fabric and four ears from the orange fabric, adding 1cm (³/₈in) all around. Cut two pocket trims (6cm (2¹/₂in) × width of the pocket) from the patterned fabric and six claws from the white felt.

(con't)

CALCULATING FABRIC LENGTHS	6 months–3 years	3–7 years
110cm (44in)	100cm (39in)	120cm (47in)
150cm (60in)	80cm (31¹/₂in)	100cm (39in)

WILD THINGS

YOKE AND POCKETS

1. Bond adhesive web to the wrong side of the patterned fabric for the inner ears. Using the inner ear template on page 203, cut two inner ears.

2. Peel the backing paper off the adhesive web and position the inner ears onto the right side of two orange ear pieces, as shown on the template. Iron to fuse into place. Using matching thread, topstitch the inner ear into place 2mm (¹/₈in) from the edges.

3. Place the ear front and back right sides together and sew 1cm (³/₈in) from the edge. Trim a small triangle shape at the tip of the ear, close to the seam, to give a neat pointed finish. Turn through and press on the reverse. Repeat with the other ear.

4. Bond adhesive web to the wrong side of a piece of brown fabric for two eyes and a nose. Using the templates on page 203, cut out two eyes and a nose.

5. For the cheeks, press the inner curved edge back by 1cm (³/₈in). Pin the cheeks on the front yoke, matching the raw edges. Stitch down with matching thread.

6. Peeling off the backing paper, apply the nose and eyes to the face. Cover with a cloth and heat press. Stitch around the edges of the eyes and nose to secure. If this gets difficult, you can simply sew horizontally, then vertically to create a cross shape to secure.

7. Place the front yoke pieces right sides together. Add interfacing if you wish. Pin the ears in place between the layers. Sew around the top curved edge 1cm (³/₈in) from the edge, trapping the ears in place as you go. Carefully snip the curved edges, then turn back through ready to add to the dress.

8. Cut two pocket trims 5cm (2¹/₂in) by the width of the pocket. Overlock, fold back and press. Overlock the remaining raw edges. Turn back the top edge by 2cm (³/₄in) and sew down. Turn back and press the remaining edges by 1cm (³/₈in). Pin the pockets into place as marked on the pattern to the dress front.

9. Then cut triangles of felt for the claws, each 4 × 2cm (1¹/₂ × ³/₄in). Insert three into position under the edge of each pocket. Sew the pockets into position all the way around 5mm (¹/₄in) from the pressed edge, making sure the claws are trapped into place as you go.

(CON'T)

SEWING TOGETHER AND MAKING STRAPS

1. Place the dress panels right sides together and sew the side seams with a 1 cm (³/₈in) seam allowance. Overlock the edges and press the seams back.

2. Make straps by placing pairs of straps right sides together and sewing around the edges by 1 cm (³/₈in), leaving the straight, narrow end open. Snip carefully around the curve, then turn through and press. Topstitch around the edges. Sew the straps into place on the back shoulders.

3. Make the two front tucks on the front, with the tucks open towards the outer edes on the right side, and sew down.

4. Pin the prepared yoke (or bib) right side facing the dress front section. Stitch it into place. Overlock the edges, turn back and press.

5. Take the back facing and finish the lower curved edge by overlocking.

6. Place the facing into position, right sides facing the back of the dress. Sew around the outer edges, trapping the shoulder straps as you go. Carefully snip into the curved edges and trim the corners. Turn through and press.

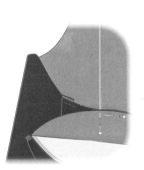

7. Slip stitch the shorter facing edges into place on the dress sides.

8. Topstitch, approximately 5mm (¹/₄in) from the edge all the way around the top edges of the dress.

FINISHING

1. Make a buttonhole (or two if you wish the strap to be adjustable) on each strap, referring to the manual of your sewing machine. Sew the buttons into place on the back of the yoke (or bib).

2. Finally, hem the dress, either by overlocking the edge, then turning back by 1 cm (³/₈in) and sewing into place, or by turning back twice to hide the raw edges. Press.

Little chick dress

An endearing little baby bird dress for babies and tots, with little duckling feet. Especially cute for little ones.

YOU WILL NEED

- Character dress patterns: front, back, yoke, strap and pocket
- Chick face template
- 1 length of soft, medium-weight, woven cotton fabric, such as corduroy, velvet, or cotton twill (see Calculating fabric lengths, below)
- Tailor's chalk
- Brown fabric for the eyes
- Orange fabric for the feet and beak
- 30cm (12in) square of iron-on, double-sided adhesive web
- Matching sewing threads
- 2 or 4 buttons

CUTTING OUT

1. Choose the best size for your child, using the guide on page 30. Trace the patterns for the Character dress in the envelope, following the lines for the correct size and the side extensions for the dress back.

2. Press the main fabric and arrange it on a flat surface so that you can cut out one front, one back, one facing, two face bibs, four straps and two pockets. Make sure the grain lines on the pattern are parallel to the selvedge and that any pile is running in the right direction.

3. If the yoke needs a little extra weight, cut another bib from plain cotton or interfacing.

4. Mark around the pattern pieces using tailor's chalk, adding 1cm (³⁄₈in) all around, but 2cm (¾in) at the hem. Cut the pieces out carefully.

(CON'T)

CALCULATING FABRIC LENGTHS	6 months–3 years	3–7 years
110cm (44in)	100cm (39in)	120cm (47in)
150cm (60in)	80cm (31 ¹⁄₂in)	100cm (39in)

WILD THINGS

YOKE AND POCKETS

1. Bond adhesive web to the fabrics for the beak and eyes. Using the template on page 204, cut out one beak and two eyes.

2. Positon the two eyes and beak on the front yoke, remove the paper backing, and press into place. Stitch to secure.

3. Place the front yoke pieces right sides together. Add interfacing if you wish. Sew around the top curved edge 1 cm (³/₈in) from the edge. Carefully snip into the curved edges, then turn through, ready to add to the dress.

4. Prepare the pockets by overlocking the edges. Turn back the top edge by 2 cm (³/₄in) and sew down.

5. Turn back and press the remaining edges by 1 cm (³/₈in). Pin the pockets on the dress front as marked on the pattern.

6. Cut four webbed feet from the orange fabric. Place two feet pieces right sides together. Sew around the curved edges 5mm (¹/₄in) from the edge. Snip into the curves, turn through and press. Repeat for the other foot. Insert these into position under each pocket edge. Sew each pocket into position all the way around 5mm (¹/₄in) from the pressed edge, making sure the feet are trapped in place as you go.

SEWING TOGETHER AND MAKING STRAPS

1. Place the dress panels right sides together and sew the side seams with a 1 cm (³/₈in) seam allowance. Overlock the edges and press the seams back.

2. Make straps by placing pairs of straps, right sides together and sewing around the edges with a 1 cm (³/₈in) seam allowance, leaving the straight narrow end open. Snip carefully around the curve, then turn through and press. Topstitch around the edges. Sew the straps into place on the back shoulders.

3. Make the two front tucks on the front, with the tucks open towards the outer edges on the right side and sew down.

4. Pin the prepared yoke (or bib) right side facing the dress front. Stitch it into place. Overlock the edges, turn back and press.

5. Take the back facing and finish the lower curved edge by overlocking.

6. Place the facing into position, right sides facing the dress back. Sew around the outer edges, trapping the shoulder straps as you go. Carefully snip the curved edges and trim excess from the corners. Turn through and press. Slip stitch the shorter facing edges into place on the dress sides.

7. Topstitch approximately 5mm (¹/₄in) from the edge all the way around.

FINISHING

1. Make a buttonhole (or two if you wish the strap to be adjustable), referring to the manual of your sewing machine. Sew the buttons into place.

2. Finally, hem the dress either by overlocking the edge, then turning back by 1 cm (³/₈in) and sewing into place, or by turning back twice to hide the raw edges.

Owl dress

This beautiful sleepy owl is made in a deep chocolate colour but works equally well in bright contrasting fabrics. Use a ditsy or spotty contrast print for the wings.

YOU WILL NEED

- Character dress patterns: front, back, yoke, strap and pocket
- Owl face template
- 1 length of soft, medium-weight, woven cotton fabric, such as corduroy, velvet, or cotton twill (see Calculating fabric lengths, below)
- Tailor's chalk
- Cotton fabric scraps in orange, patterned, and brown
- Cream felt scraps
- 30cm (12in) square of iron-on, double-sided adhesive web
- 17cm (6¾in) narrow elastic
- Matching sewing threads
- 2 or 4 buttons

CUTTING OUT

1. Choose the best size for your child, using the guide on page 30. Trace the patterns for the Character dress in the envelope, following the lines for the correct size and the side extensions for the dress back.

2. Press the main fabric and arrange it on a flat surface so that you can cut out one front, one back, one facing, two face yokes (or bibs) and four straps. Make sure the grain lines on the pattern are parallel to the selvedge and that any pile is running in the right direction. For the contrast wings, draw a line on the pattern from the tuck position to approximately two-thirds down the side of the dress. Use this template to cut one pair of contrast wings.

3. Mark around the pattern pieces using tailor's chalk, adding 1cm (³⁄₈in) all around, but 2cm (³⁄₄in) at the hem. Cut the pieces out carefully.

4. If the yoke needs a little extra weight, cut another bib from plain cotton or interfacing.

(CON'T)

CALCULATING FABRIC LENGTHS	6 months–3 years	3–7 years
110cm (44in)	100cm (39in)	120cm (47in)
150cm (60in)	80cm (31½in)	100cm (39in)

YOKE, POCKETS AND WINGS

1. Bond adhesive web to the fabrics for the beak and eye components (see main photograph). Using the template on page 205, cut out the pieces for two eyes and one beak. Peeling off the backing paper, position the features on the yoke and sew into place.

2. Using the template, cut out four ear pieces, adding 1cm (³/₈in) all around. Place two pieces right sides together and sew 1cm (³/₈in) from the edge. Trim a small triangle shape at the tip of the ear, close to the seam, to give a neat pointed finish. Turn through and press on the reverse. Repeat with the other ear.

3. Place the front yoke pieces right sides together. Add interfacing if you wish. Pin the ears in place between the layers. Sew around the top curved edge 1cm (³/₈in) from the edge, trapping the ears in place as you go. Carefully snip into the curved edges, then turn through, ready to add to the dress.

4. Prepare the pouch pocket by overlocking the edges. Turn back the top edge by 2cm (³/₄in) and sew down, creating a channel. Use a safety pin to thread the elastic through, gather and secure at the ends.

5. Turn back and press the remaining edges by 1cm (³/₈in). Pin the pocket into place on the dress, as marked.

6. Using the template on page 205, cut two felt feet. Insert these into position under the pocket edge. Sew the pocket into position all the way around, 5mm (¹/₄in) from the pressed edge, making sure the feet are trapped into place as you go.

7. Cut out two wings from patterned fabric. Press under 1cm (³/₈in) around the curved edge of each piece. Pin the wrong side of the wings to the right side of the dress front, matching the raw edges. Sew in place and press.

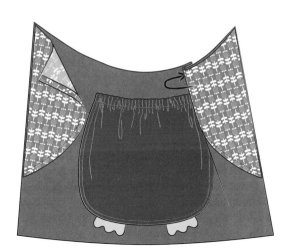

SEWING TOGETHER AND MAKING STRAPS

1. Place the dress panels right sides together and sew the side seams with a 1cm (³⁄₈in) seam allowance. Overlock the edges and press the seams back.

2. Make the straps by placing pairs of straps with right sides together and sewing around the edges with a 1cm (³⁄₈in) seam allowance, leaving the straight narrow end open. Snip carefully into the curve, then turn through and press. Topstitch around the edges. Sew the straps into place at the back shoulders.

3. Make the two front tucks on the front, with the tucks open towards the outer edges on the right side and sew down. Pin the prepared yoke right side facing the front of the dress. Stitch it into place.

4. Take the back facing and finish the lower curved edge by overlocking.

5. Place the facing into position, right sides facing the dress back. Sew around the outer edges, trapping the shoulder straps as you go. Carefully snip the curved edges and trim excess from the corners. Turn through and press. Slip stitch the shorter facing edges into place on the dress sides.

6. Topstitch approximately 5mm (¹⁄₄in) from the edge all the way around.

FINISHING

1. Make a buttonhole (or two if you wish the strap to be adjustable), referring to the manual of your sewing machine. Sew the buttons into place.

2. Finally, hem the dress either by overlocking the edge, then turning back by 1cm (³⁄₈in) and sewing into place, or by turning back twice to hide the raw edges.

Baby mouse dress

This little mouse is a classic. It has a charming, very British quality to it, and looks lovely with small floral or tiny spot prints in the ears and on the pockets. It's perfect for babies too.

YOU WILL NEED

- Character dress patterns: front back, yoke, strap and pocket
- Mouse face template
- 1 length of soft, medium-weight, grey woven cotton fabric, such as corduroy, velvet, or cotton twill (see Calculating fabric lengths, below)
- Tailor's chalk
- Black fabric for the eyes and whiskers
- Pink for the nose and ears
- Contrast pink or spot fabric for the pocket edges and inner ear, if desired
- White felt scraps
- 30cm (12in) square of iron-on, double-sided adhesive web
- Matching sewing threads
- 2 or 4 buttons

CUTTING OUT

1. Choose the best size for your child, using the guide on page 30. Trace the patterns for the Character dress in the envelope, following the lines for the correct size and the side extensions for the dress back.

2. Press the main fabric and arrange it on a flat surface so that you can cut out one front, one back, one facing, two face yokes (or bibs), four straps and two pockets. Make sure the grain lines on the pattern are parallel to the selvedge and that any pile is running in the right direction.

3. Mark around the pattern pieces using tailor's chalk, adding 1 cm (³/₈in) all around, but 2 cm (³/₄in) at the hem. Cut the pieces out carefully.

4. If the yoke needs a little extra weight, cut another bib from plain cotton or interfacing.

(CON'T)

CALCULATING FABRIC LENGTHS	6 months–3 years	3–7 years
110cm (44in)	100cm (39in)	120cm (47in)
150cm (60in)	80cm (31 ½in)	100cm (39in)

YOKE

1. Using the template on page 206, cut four grey ears, adding 1 cm (³/₈in) all around.

2. Bond adhesive web to the wrong side of the fabric for the inner ears and other face features.

3. Using the template, cut two inner ears and the other face features.

4. Peeling off the backing paper, arrange the features on the face panel, cover with a soft cloth and press into place. Topstitch around the edges with matching thread. If this gets difficult, you can simply sew horizontally, then vertically to create a cross shape to secure.

5. Bond the inner ears to two of the ear pieces. Topstitch in place.

6. Place an ear front and back right sides together and sew 1 cm (³/₈in) from the edge. Carefully snip into the curved edges. Turn through, press, and repeat for the second ear.

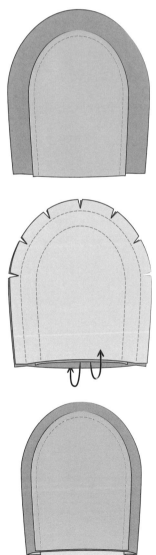

POCKETS

1. Cut two pocket trims 5cm (2½in) by the width of the pocket. Overlock, fold back and press. Overlock the remaining raw edges. Turn back the top edge by 2cm (¾in) and sew down. Turn back and press the remaining edges by 1cm (⅜in). Pin the pockets into place as marked on the pattern to the dress front.

2. Then cut triangles of felt for the claws, each 4 × 2cm (1½ × ¾in). Insert three into position under the edge of each pocket.

3. Sew the pockets into position all the way around 5mm (¼in) from the pressed edge, making sure the claws are trapped into place as you go.

SEWING TOGETHER AND MAKING STRAPS

1. Place the dress panels right sides together and sew the side seams with a 1cm (⅜in) seam allowance. Overlock the edges and press the seams back.

2. Make straps by placing pairs of straps, right sides together and sewing around the edges with a 1cm (⅜in) seam allowance, leaving the straight narrow end open. Snip carefully around the curve, then turn through and press. Topstitch around the edges. Sew the straps into place on the back shoulders.

3. Make the two front tucks on the front, with the tucks open towards the outer edges on the right side and sew down.

4. Pin the prepared yoke (or bib) right side facing the dress front. Stitch it into place. Overlock the edges, turn back and press.

5. Take the back facing and finish the lower curved edge by overlocking.

6. Place the facing into position, right sides facing the dress back. Sew around the outer edges, trapping the shoulder straps as you go. Carefully snip the curved edges and trim excess from the corners. Turn through and press. Slip stitch the shorter facing edges into place on the dress sides.

7. Topstitch approximately 5mm (¼in) from the edge all the way around.

FINISHING

1. Make a buttonhole (or two if you wish the strap to be adjustable), referring to the manual of your sewing machine. Sew the buttons into place.

2. Finally, hem the dress, either by overlocking the edge, then turning back by 1cm (⅜in) and sewing into place, or by turning back twice to hide the raw edges.

Mr Bear dungarees

This Mr Bear dungaree set for boys (or girls) has a beautiful soft character face, sure to be an all-time favourite. The dungaree pattern can be used to create a number of character designs using different faces as a starting point. The simple patch pockets have soft felt claws, making the dungaree perfect for role play and bear hunting!

YOU WILL NEED

- ⊕ Character dungaree, yoke, strap and pocket patterns
- ⊕ Bear face template
- ⊕ Brown medium-weight fabric (see Calculating fabric lengths, below)
- ⊕ Tailor's chalk
- ⊕ Contrast fabric for the facings, backs of straps and turnups
- ⊕ Cotton fabric scraps in cream and brown
- ⊕ Contrast fabric for the pockets, enough for two squares approx. 15cm (6in)
- ⊕ Cream felt scraps for the claws
- ⊕ 30cm (12in) square of iron-on, double-sided adhesive web
- ⊕ Matching sewing threads
- ⊕ 2 or 4 buttons

CUTTING OUT

1. Choose the best size for your child, using the guide below. Trace the patterns for the Dungarees in the envelope, following the lines for the correct size, the yoke and the turnup seam.

2. Press the main fabric and arrange it on a flat surface so you can cut out two dungaree front/backs, one yoke (or bib) and two straps. Make sure the grain line is parallel to the selvedge and that any pile is running in the right direction.

3. Mark around the pattern pieces using tailor's chalk, adding 1cm (³/₈in) all around. Cut the pieces out carefully.

4. Using the dungaree pattern and adding seam allowances all around, cut the bib facing, back facing, two straps and two turnups from contrast fabric. If the yoke needs a little extra weight, cut another bib from plain cotton or interfacing.

(CON'T)

SIZE GUIDE

Age	Height
6–18 months	to 80cm (31 ½in)
18 months–3 years	to 98cm (39in)
3–5 years	to 110cm (43in)

CALCULATING FABRIC LENGTHS

	6 months–3 years	3–5 years
110cm (44in)	120cm (47in)	140cm (55in)
150cm (60in)	100cm (39in)	120 cm (47in)

YOKE, POCKETS AND BOTTOM PATCH

1. Using the bear face template on page 207, cut four brown ears, adding 1cm (³/₈in) all around.

2. Bond adhesive web to the wrong side of the fabric for the inner ears and other face features.

3. Using the template, cut two inner ears and the other face features.

4. Peeling off the backing paper, arrange the features on the face panel, cover with a soft cloth and press into place. Topstitch around the edges with matching thread.

5. Bond the inner ears to two of the brown ear pieces. Topstitch in place.

6. Place an ear front and back right sides together and sew 1cm (³/₈in) from the edge. Carefully snip into the curved edges. Turn through, press, and repeat for the second ear.

7. Place the yoke pieces right sides together. Add interfacing if you wish. Pin the ears in place between the yoke. Sew around the top curved edge 1cm (3/8in) from the edge, trapping the ears as you go. Carefully snip into the curved edges, then turn through and press ready to add to the dungarees.

8. Cut two pockets from contrast fabric. Overlock the edges. Turn back the top edge by 2cm (³/₄in) and sew down. Turn back and press the remaining edges by 1cm (³/₈in). Pin the pockets into place as marked on the pattern on the dungaree fronts.

9. Then cut six claws from triangles of felt for the claws, each 4 × 2cm (1¹/₂ × ³/₄in). Insert three into position under the edge of each pocket. Sew the pockets into position all the way around 5mm (¹/₄in) from the pressed edge, making sure the claws are trapped into place as you go.

10. Cut two bottom patch panels from the main or contrast fabric, using the shape on the Dungaree pattern. Turn back the curved edges and press. Pin the panels into place on the dungarees as marked on the pattern, then topstitch down. Adding the bottom patch makes a lovely detail, especially for little crawlers, and also adds a layer of durability.

SEWING SEAMS TOGETHER AND MAKING STRAPS

1. Place the dungaree panels right sides together and sew the centre front and centre back seams with a 1cm (³/₈in) seam allowance. It's worth stitching the back seam twice to be extra hard-wearing. Overlock the edges and press the seams back.

2. Place one contrast turnup strip along the hem edge with right sides facing and sew along the hemline. Overlock and press open. Overlock the hem edge.

3. Sew the inside leg seams from one hem to the other, including the turnups. Overlock the edges. Fold the turnup under, pin and stitch it in place along the existing seam line. Repeat for the other turnup.

4. Make straps by placing main fabric and facing right sides together and sewing around the edges with a 1cm (³/₈in) seam allowance, leaving the straight narrow end open. Snip carefully around the curve, then turn through and press the straps. Sew the straps into place on the back shoulders so they will cross over the back when fastened.

5. Make the two front tucks on the front, with the tucks open towards the outer edges on the right side, and sew down.

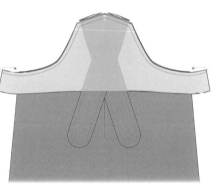

6. Pin the prepared yoke (or bib) right side facing the front section. Stitch it into place. Overlock the edges, turn back and press.

7. Take the back facing and finish the lower curved edge by overlocking.

8. Place the facing into position, right sides facing the back. Sew around the outer edges, trapping the shoulder straps as you go. Carefully snip the curved edges and trim excess from the corners. Turn through and press. Slip stitch the shorter facing edges into place on the dungaree sides.

FINISHING

1. Topstitch approximately 5mm (¹/₄in) from the edge all the way around.

2. Make a buttonhole (or two if you wish the strap to be adjustable), referring to the manual of your sewing machine. Sew the buttons into place on the back of the bib.

Puppy dog dungarees

These fun puppy dog dungarees can be made in almost any colour. Using lightweight denim gives them a real utility feel. I've used a cotton cord that is durable while having a lovely soft feel. Add a star in a bright shade and contrast trims to personalise.

YOU WILL NEED

- Character dungaree, yoke, strap and pocket patterns
- Puppy dog template
- Medium-weight cotton fabric, such as corduroy or cotton twill (see Calculating fabric lengths, below)
- Tailor's chalk
- Contrast fabric for the facings, backs of straps and turnups
- Cotton fabric scraps in cream, black, a darker shade for the muzzle and patterned for the inner ear
- 30cm (12in) square of iron-on, double-sided adhesive web
- Matching sewing threads
- 2 or 4 buttons

CUTTING OUT

1. Choose the best size for your child, using the guide below. Trace the patterns for the Dungarees in the envelope, following the lines for the correct size, the yoke and the turnup seam.

2. Press the main fabric and arrange it on a flat surface so you can cut out two dungaree front/backs, one yoke (or bib), two pockets and two straps. Make sure the grain line is parallel to the selvedge and that any pile is running in the right direction.

3. Mark around the pattern pieces using tailor's chalk, adding 1cm (³/₈in) all around. Cut the pieces out carefully.

4. Using the dungaree pattern and adding seam allowances all around, cut the bib facing, back facing, two straps and two turnups from contrast fabric. If the yoke needs a little extra weight, cut another bib from plain cotton or interfacing.

(CON'T)

SIZE GUIDE

Age	Height
6–18 months	to 80cm (31 ½in)
18 months–3 years	to 98cm (39in)
3–5 years	to 110cm (43in)

CALCULATING FABRIC LENGTHS

	6 months–3 years	3–5 years
110cm (44in)	120cm (47in)	140cm (55in)
150cm (60in)	100cm (39in)	120cm (47in)

WILD THINGS

YOKE, POCKETS AND BOTTOM PATCH

1. Using the puppy face template on page 208, cut two ears from the main fabric, adding 1cm (³⁄₈in) all around. Cut another two from the contrast fabric.

2. Prepare the fabric for the contrast features by pressing web to the reverse. Using the template, mark the shapes on the paper side of the fabric and cut the face shapes (see image right as a guide).

3. Peeling off the backing paper, arrange the features on the face panel, cover with a soft cloth and press into place. Topstitch close to the edges.

4. Place the ear front and back right sides together and sew 1cm (³⁄₈in) from the edge. Carefully snip into the curved edges. Turn through, press, and repeat for the second ear.

5. Place the yoke pieces right sides together. Add interfacing if you wish. Pin the ears in place between the yoke. Sew around the top curved edge 1cm (3/8in) from the edge, trapping the ears as you go. Carefully snip into the curved edges, then turn through and press ready to add to the dungarees.

6. Prepare the pockets by overlocking the edges. Position the coloured star on one of the pockets. Bond and topstitch in place.

7. Turn back the top edge by 2cm (³⁄₄in) and sew down. Turn back and press the remaining edges by 1cm (³⁄₈in). Pin the pockets into place as marked on the pattern on the dungaree fronts.

8. Sew the pockets into position all the way around 5mm (¹⁄₄in) from the pressed edge.

9. Cut two bottom patch panels from the main or contrast fabric, using the shape on the Dungaree pattern. Turn back the curved edges and press. Pin the panels into place on the dungarees as marked on the pattern, the topstitch down. Adding the bottom patch makes a lovely detail, especially for little crawlers, and also adds a layer of durability.

(CON'T)

SEWING SEAMS TOGETHER AND MAKING STRAPS

1. Place the dungaree panels right sides together and sew the centre front and centre back seams with a 1cm (³/₈in) seam allowance. It's worth stitching the back seam twice to be extra hard-wearing. Overlock the edges and press the seams back.

2. Place one contrast turnup strip along the hem edge with right sides facing and sew along the hemline. Overlock and press open. Overlock the hem edge.

3. Sew the inside leg seams from one hem to the other, including the turnups. Overlock the edges. Fold the turnup under, pin and stitch it in place along the existing seam line. Repeat for the other turnup.

4. Make straps by placing main fabric and facing right sides together and sewing around the edges with a 1cm (³/₈in) seam allowance, leaving the straight narrow end open. Snip carefully around the curve, then turn through and press the straps. Sew the straps into place on the back shoulders so they will cross over the back when fastened.

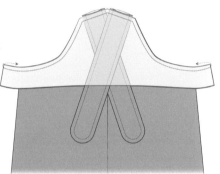

5. Make the two front tucks on the front, with the tucks open towards the outer edges on the right side, and sew down.

6. Pin the prepared yoke (or bib) right side facing the front section. Stitch it into place. Overlock the edges, turn back and press.

7. Take the back facing and finish the lower curved edge by overlocking.

8. Place the facing into position, right sides facing the back. Sew around the outer edges, trapping the shoulder straps as you go. Carefully snip the curved edges and trim excess from the corners. Turn through and press. Slip stitch the shorter facing edges into place on the dungaree sides.

FINISHING

1. Topstitch approximately 5mm (¹/₄in) from the edge all the way around.

2. Make a buttonhole (or two if you wish the strap to be adjustable), referring to the manual of your sewing machine. Sew the buttons into place on the back of the bib.

Sunshine or rainbow dungarees

These dungarees for boys and girls are happy, bright and extremely practical. Choose a sturdy fabric such as corduroy, twill or denim.

YOU WILL NEED

- Character dungaree, yoke, strap and pocket patterns
- Sunshine or rainbow template
- Medium-weight woven cotton fabric, such as corduroy or cotton twill (see Calculating fabric lengths, below)
- Tailor's chalk
- Approx. 25cm (10in) contrast print or plain fabric for the facings, backs of straps and turnups
- Cotton fabric scraps in bright rainbow colours, including yellow for the face
- 30cm (12in) square iron-on, double-sided adhesive web
- Matching sewing threads
- 2 or 4 buttons

CUTTING OUT

1. Choose the best size for your child, using the guide below. Trace the patterns for the Dungarees in the envelope, following the lines for the correct size, the yoke and the turnup seam.

2. Press the main fabric and arrange it on a flat surface so you can cut out two dungaree front/backs, one yoke (or bib), two pockets and two straps. Make sure the grain line is parallel to the selvedge and that any pile is running in the right direction.

3. Mark around the pattern pieces using tailor's chalk, adding 1cm (³⁄₈in) all around. Cut the pieces out carefully.

4. Using the dungaree pattern and adding seam allowances all around, cut the bib facing, back facing, two straps and two turnups from contrast fabric. If the yoke needs a little extra weight, cut another bib from plain cotton or interfacing.

(CON'T)

SIZE GUIDE	
Age	**Height**
6–18 months	to 80cm (31 ½in)
18 months–3 years	to 98cm (39in)
3–5 years	to 110cm (43in)

CALCULATING FABRIC LENGTHS	6 months–3 years	3–5 years
110cm (44in)	120cm (47in)	140cm (55in)
150cm (60in)	100cm (39in)	120cm (47in)

YOKE AND POCKETS

1. Using the sunshine or rainbow template on pages 209/210, prepare the fabric for your chosen design by pressing web to the reverse. Using the template, mark the shapes on the paper side of the fabric and cut them out.

2. Peeling off the backing paper, arrange the features on the bib. Cover with a soft cloth and press into place. Topstitch close to the edges.

3. Place the bib pieces right sides together. Add interfacing if you wish. Sew around the top curved edge 1cm (3/8in) from the edge, trapping the ears as you go. Carefully snip into the curved edges, then turn through and press ready to add to the dungarees.

4. Prepare the pockets by overlocking the edges. Turn back the top edge by 1.5cm (⁵/₈in) and sew down. Turn back and press the remaining edges by 1cm (³/₈in). Repeat the appliqué process to apply clouds or little raindrops to the pockets.

5. Pin the pockets into place as marked on the pattern on the dungaree fronts.

6. Sew the pockets into position all the way around 2mm (¹/₈in) from the pressed edge, making sure you backstitch or reinforce with a small triangle at the start and finish.

SEWING SEAMS TOGETHER AND MAKING STRAPS

1. Place the dungaree panels right sides together and sew the centre front and centre back seams with a 1cm (³/₈in) seam allowance. It's worth stitching the back seam twice to be extra hard-wearing. Overlock the edges and press the seams back.

2. Place one contrast turnup strip along the hem edge with right sides facing and sew along the hemline. Overlock and press open. Overlock the hem edge.

3. Sew the inside leg seams from one hem to the other, including the turnups. Overlock the edges. Fold the turnup under, pin and stitch it in place along the existing seam line. Repeat for the other turnup.

4. Make straps by placing main fabric and facing right sides together and sewing around the edges with a 1cm (³/₈in) seam allowance, leaving the straight narrow end open. Snip carefully around the curve, then turn through and press the straps. Sew the straps into place on the back shoulders so they will cross over the back when fastened.

5. Make the two front tucks on the front, with the tucks open towards the outer edges on the right side, and sew down.

6. Pin the prepared yoke (or bib) right side facing the front section. Stitch it into place. Overlock the edges, turn back and press.

7. Take the back facing and finish the lower curved edge by overlocking. Place the facing into position, right sides facing the back. Sew around the outer edges, trapping the shoulder straps as you go. Carefully snip the curved edges and trim excess from the corners. Turn through and press. Slip stitch the shorter facing edges into place on the dungaree sides.

FINISHING

1. Topstitch approximately 5mm (¹/₄in) from the edge all the way around.

2. Make a buttonhole (or two if you wish the strap to be adjustable), referring to the manual of your sewing machine. Sew the buttons into place on the back of the bib.

Mr or Mrs Wolf dungarees

This playful character is perfect for role play and fairytale themed parties. I've used a cotton cord which is durable while having a lovely soft feel and a funky contrast printed fabric for the ears and trims. It works equally well with soft ditsy prints inside the ears for Mrs Wolf. The face is the same as for the fox, making the template really versatile.

YOU WILL NEED

- ⊕ Character dungaree, yolk, strap and pocket patterns
- ⊕ Wolf face template
- ⊕ Medium-weight woven cotton fabric, such as corduroy or cotton twill (see Calculating fabric lengths, below)
- ⊕ Tailor's chalk (optional) or soft pencil
- ⊕ Contrast print fabric for the inside facings, ears and turnups
- ⊕ Plain tonal fabric for the bottom patch and face features
- ⊕ Cotton fabric scraps in cream for the cheeks
- ⊕ 30cm (12in) square iron-on, double-sided bonding web
- ⊕ White felt scraps
- ⊕ Matching sewing threads
- ⊕ 2 or 4 buttons

SIZE GUIDE

Age	Height
6–18 months	to 80cm (31 ½in)
18 months–3 years	to 98cm (39in)
3–5 years	to 110cm (43in)

CALCULATING FABRIC LENGTHS

	6 months–3 years	3–5 years
110cm (44in)	120cm (47in)	140cm (55in)
150cm (60in)	100cm (39in)	120cm (47in)

CUTTING OUT

1. Choose the best size for your child, using the guide on page 163. Trace the patterns for the Dungarees in the envelope, following the lines for the correct size, the yoke and the turnup seam.

2. Press the main fabric and arrange it on a flat surface so you can cut out two dungaree front/backs, one yoke (or bib), two pockets and four straps. Make sure the grain line is parallel to the selvedge and that any pile is running in the right direction. You may wish to strengthen the face by adding a third layer of plain cotton or interfacing between the two face pieces.

3. Mark around the pattern pieces using tailor's chalk, adding 1cm (³/₈in) all around. Cut the pieces out carefully.

4. Using the dungaree pattern and adding seam allowances all around, cut the bib facing, back facing and two turnups from contrast fabric. If the yoke needs a little extra weight, cut another bib from plain cotton or interfacing.

FACE AND POCKETS

1. Bond adhesive web to the wrong side of the patterned fabric for the inner ears. Using the inner ear template on page 203, cut two inner ears.

2. Peel the backing paper off the adhesive web and position the inner ears onto the right side of the main fabric ear pieces, as shown on the template. Iron to fuse into place. Using matching thread, topstitch the inner ear into place 2mm (¹/₈in) from the edges.

3. Place the ear front and back right sides together and sew 1cm (³/₈in) from the edge. Trim a small triangle shape at the tip of the ear, close to the seam, to give a neat pointed finish. Turn through and press on the reverse. Repeat with the other ear.

4. Bond adhesive web to the wrong side of a piece of dark fabric for two eyes and a nose. Using the templates on page 203, cut out two eyes and a nose.

5. For the cheeks, press the inner curved edge back by 1cm (³/₈in). Pin the cheeks on the front yoke, matching the raw edges. Stitch down with matching thread.

6. Peeling off the backing paper, apply the nose and eyes to the face. Cover with a cloth and heat press. Stitch around the edges of the eyes and nose to secure.

7. Place the front yoke pieces right sides together. Add interfacing if you wish. Pin the ears in place between the layers. Sew around the top curved edge 1cm (³/₈in) from the edge, trapping the ears in place as you go. Carefully snip the curved edges, then turn back through ready to add to the dungarees.

(CON'T)

8. Prepare the pockets by overlocking the edges. Turn back the top edge by 2cm (³⁄₄in) and sew down. Turn back and press the remaining edges by 1cm (³⁄₈in). Pin the pockets into place as marked on the pattern on the dungaree front.

9. Then cut six triangles of felt for the claws, each 4 × 2cm (1½ × ³⁄₄in). Insert three into position under the edge of each pocket. Sew the pockets into position all the way around 5mm (¹⁄₄in) from the pressed edge, making sure the claws are trapped into place as you go.

BOTTOM PATCH

Cut two bottom patch panels from the main or contrast fabric, using the shape on the Dungaree pattern. Turn back the curved edges and press. Pin the panels into place on the dungarees as marked on the pattern, then topstitch down. Adding the bottom patch makes a lovely detail, especially for little crawlers, and also adds a layer of durability.

SEWING SEAMS TOGETHER AND MAKING STRAPS

1. Place the dungaree panels right sides together and sew the centre front and centre back seams with a 1cm (⅜in) seam allowance. It's worth stitching the back seam twice to be extra hard-wearing. Overlock the edges and press the seams back.

2. Place one contrast turnup strip along the hem edge with right sides facing and sew along the hemline. Overlock and press open. Overlock the hem edge.

3. Sew the inside leg seams from one hem to the other, including the turnups. Overlock the edges. Fold the turnup under, pin and stitch it in place along the existing seam line. Repeat for the other turnup.

4. Make straps by placing main fabric and facing right sides together and sewing around the edges with a 1cm (⅜in) seam allowance, leaving the straight narrow end open. Snip carefully around the curve, then turn through and press the straps. Sew the straps into place on the back shoulders so they will cross over the back when fastened.

5. Make the two front tucks on the front, with the tucks open towards the outer edges on the right side, and sew down.

6. Pin the prepared yoke (or bib) right side facing the front section. Stitch it into place. Overlock the edges, turn back and press.

7. Take the back facing and finish the lower curved edge by overlocking. Place the facing into position, right sides facing the back. Sew around the outer edges, trapping the shoulder straps as you go. Carefully snip the curved edges and trim excess from the corners. Turn through and press. Slip stitch the shorter facing edges into place on the dungaree sides.

FINISHING

1. Topstitch approximately 5mm (¼in) from the edge all the way around.

2. Make a buttonhole (or two if you wish the strap to be adjustable), referring to the manual of your sewing machine. Sew the buttons into place on the back of the bib.

Fairy-tale cape

This gorgeous cape finishes off that special party dress, and will be a favourite dress-up piece too. It has a beautiful folklore look and a delightful pointed hood, which on its own, also makes a stunning baby bonnet (see page 172).

YOU WILL NEED

- Cape front, back and side, and hood patterns
- 120cm (48in) velvet or cord fabric, 110cm (44in) or wider
- 120cm (48in) lining fabric, 110cm (44in) or wider
- Tailor's chalk
- Matching sewing threads
- Ric rac braid (optional)
- 1 button, 2cm (¾in) in diameter

CUTTING OUT

1. Choose the best size for your child, using the guide on page 30. Trace the pattern for the Cape front, Cape back, Cape side and Cape hood on the web (see page 11), following the lines for the correct size.

2. Mark around the pattern pieces using tailor's chalk, adding 1cm (⅜in) all around. Cut the pieces out carefully.

ASSEMBLING THE CAPE AND HOOD

1. Place the two main hood pieces right sides together and sew along the top and centre back with a 1cm (⅜in) seam allowance. Trim the excess at the corner and press. Repeat for the hood.

2. Place the hood and lining right sides together and sew around the front edge. Press and turn through. Press again.

3. If desired, sew ric rac on the right side of the hood around the front edge, 2cm (¾in) from the edge.

4. Make a rouleau loop (see page 26) from the main fabric that is large enough to comfortably fit over the button you wish to use.

5. Sew a side panel to each front panel, right sides together, leaving an opening for the hand openings. Press the seams open.

6. Sew the side panels to the back panel, right sides together. Press open.

7. Pin the hood and sew into place to the neck edge of the cape, right sides together with a 1cm (⅜in) seam allowance. Make sure the front edges of the hood and the cape align. Snip into the seam allowance as necessary to press the seam open.

(CON'T)

WILD THINGS

ASSEMBLING THE LINING

1. Make the cape lining in the same way and press. Sew it to the hood lining but leave an opening at the back large enough to turn the cape through later. Press.

2. Place the main cape and lining right sides together. Position the rouleau loop at the top front of the edge. Sew all the way around, trapping the rouleau loop.

3. Carefully snip across the corners to give a neat finish, then pull the cape through the openings in the neck seam. Carefully press.

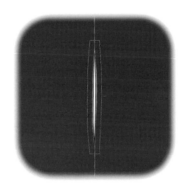

TIP
If you are using a velvet fabric as I have, always press gently on the reverse, as too much pressure will damage the pile of the velvet.

FINISHING

1. Position the armhole openings in the main cape and lining wrong sides together with the seam allowances turned in. Pin, then tack into place. Sew 5mm (¼in) all around each opening.

2. Neatly stitch the opening in the hood neck seam closed.

3. If desired, complete by sewing ric rac 2cm (¾in) above the hemline and stitching the button into place.

Fairy-tale bonnet

I love the shape of this beautiful baby bonnet, which has a lovely Scandinavian fairy-tale feel about it. It's super-easy to make, using the cape hood pattern. Made here in red velvet and trimmed with ric rac, you might like to try adding contrast woven braid to the edges too.

YOU WILL NEED

- Cape hood pattern
- 25cm (10in) fabric
- 25cm (10in) lining
- Fabric for bias binding, 60 × 5cm (24 × 2in)
- Ric rac braid (optional)
- Matching sewing threads

1. Trace the pattern for the Cape hood on the web (see page 11), following the lines for the correct size. Cut two hood pieces, making sure any pile runs in the correct direction. Repeat for the lining.

2. Make the hood, following steps 1–3 on page 168. Once assembled, make two tucks in the centre back the neckline edge to 32cm (12¾in).

3. Cut the strip of fabric for the bias binding. Press in both long edges to the centre line. Working from the centre outwards, pin and sew the binding into place along the bottom edge of the hood.

4. Sew the remaining binding edges together to create ties.

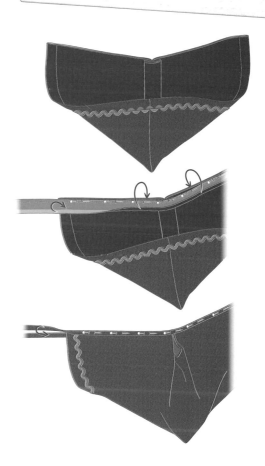

Sleepy lion jacket

This jacket is perfect for little boys and girls. The face has a lovely 70s feel, reminiscent of Maurice Sendak's illustrations of Pierre and the Lion, a family favourite. Make it in a rich gold colour with an interesting print for the mane if you can.

YOU WILL NEED

- Jacket, jacket sleeve, hood gusset, face and side, and pocket patterns
- Sleepy Lion face template
- 150cm (60in) soft, warm fabric for the body, 110cm (44in) or wider
- 150cm (60in) plain cotton or microfleece for the lining, 110cm (44in) or wider
- Tailor's chalk
- Contrast fabric for the pockets and elbow patches
- Fabric scraps for the mane, inner ears and face features
- Iron-on, double-sided adhesive web
- Felt for the claws
- Matching sewing threads
- 4 buttons

CUTTING OUT

1. Choose the best size for your child, using the guide on page 30. Trace the pattern for the Jacket, making a pattern for the front, with the neck sitting lower and the bottom edge straight, and another for the back with the lower curved bottom edge. Also trace patterns for the Jacket sleeve, Hood gusset, Hood face and Hood side on the web (see page 11), following the lines for the correct size.

2. Press the fabric, arrange it on a flat surface and place the pattern pieces on the fabric so you can cut one back, two fronts, two sleeves, and for the hood, one gusset, one face and two sides. Make sure the grain lines on the pattern are parallel to the selvedge and that any pile runs in the correct direction. Repeat for the lining.

3. Cut two pockets and two elbow patches from contrast fabric.

FACE

1. Using the template on page 211, cut out four ears from contrast fabric, adding 1cm (³⁄₈in) all around.

2. Place these pieces in pairs right sides together and sew around the curved edges with a 5mm (¼in) seam allowance. Carefully snip around the curve, then turn through and press.

3. Prepare the appliqué by backing the fabric for the inner ears and features with adhesive web.

4. Trace the shapes on the paper side and cut out two inner ears, two eyes, a nose and six whiskers.

5. Peeling off the paper backing, arrange the features on the face panel and the inner ears in place, cover with a soft cloth and press into place. Finish by topstitching with matching thread to fix in place.

6. Position and sew the ears on the top edge of the face panel, adding a tuck in the centre of each ear. Then position and sew the mane circles into place.

(CON'T)

ASSEMBLING THE HOOD

1. Pin and sew the left and right hood sides to the gusset (or centre panel), right sides together with a 1cm (³/₈in) seam allowance. Press the seams open. Attach the top edge of the face to the front edges of the sides and gusset in the same way, right sides together.

2. Repeat for the hood lining.

3. Place the main hood and lining right sides together and sew all the way around the front edges. Snip into the curved edges as required and turn through.

4. Press, rolling gently to obtain a good finish at the curved edges.

5. Finish by topstitching 5mm (¼in) from the edge all the way around the front edge.

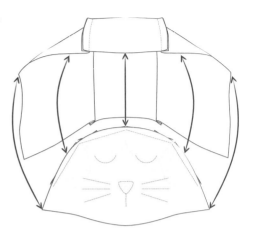

POCKETS AND ELBOW PATCHES

1. Overlock all around the pocket pieces. Turn the top edge back twice by 2cm (³/₄in) and stitch in place. Turn the remaining edges under by 1cm (³/₈in) and press.

2. Cut six triangles of felt for the claws, each 4 × 2cm (1½ × ³/₄in). Insert three into position under the edge of each pocket. Pin then sew the pockets into position all the way around 5mm (¼in) from the pressed edge, making sure the claws are trapped into place as you go. Backstitch or reinforce with a small triangle at the start and finish.

3. Cut two oval shapes for the elbow patches, approximately 11 × 13cm (4¼in × 5in). Turn the edges under 5mm (¼in) or overlock. Place one on each sleeve, halfway between the cuff and the top of the back sleeve. Topstitch into place.

SEWING TOGETHER

1. Pin the fronts and back right sides together at the shoulders and sew a 1cm (³⁄₈in) seam. Press each seam towards the back of the garment. Topstitch the jacket and seam allowance 5mm (¹⁄₄in) from the seam to strengthen and finish.

2. Working with the jacket flat, pin and sew the sleeves into place, right sides together. Press the seam allowance down towards the sleeve. Topstitch the sleeve and seam allowance 5mm (¹⁄₄in) from the seam to strengthen and finish.

3. Sew the side and sleeve seams and press.

4. Pin the bottom edge of the main hood to the neckline of the jacket, matching notches and allowing the hood to fall short of each front edge on the jacket by 2cm (³⁄₄in) edge. Carefully snip the seam allowance and press.

5. Repeat steps 1–4 for the lining. Turn the lining inside out and position right sides together over the top of the main jacket. Sew the two together around the front of the hood, fronts and hemline, leaving a gap of around 20cm (8in) at the hemline. Carefully cut excess at the front corners, then turn through. Press carefully to give a good finish, then topstitch all around 5mm (¹⁄₄in) from the edge, enclosing the opening at the hemline as you go.

6. To finish the cuffs, carefully press back the lining and main cuff by 1.5cm (5/8in). Align the edges, pin, then topstitch 5mm (¹⁄₄in) from the edge. Press.

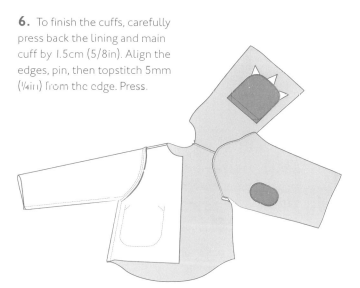

FINISHING

1. Mark the position of the buttonholes from the pattern, and referring to your sewing machine manual, carefully make four buttonholes. (Practise on some layered fabric first, if you want.)

2. Sew the buttons into place.

Bear jacket

If you're feeling a little more ambitious, this jacket shape is perfect for all year round and adds a new dimension to trips to the park and walks in the woods for your little adventurer.

YOU WILL NEED

- Jacket, jacket sleeve, hood gusset, face and side, and pocket patterns
- Bear face template
- 150cm (60in) soft, warm fabric for the body, 110cm (44in) or wider
- 150cm (60in) plain cotton or microfleece for the lining, 110cm (44in) or wider
- Tailor's chalk (optional)
- Fabric scraps for the inner ears and face features
- Contrast fabric for the pockets and elbow patches
- Iron-on, double-sided adhesive web
- Felt for the claws
- Matching sewing threads
- 4 buttons

CUTTING OUT

1. Choose the best size for your child, using the guide on page 30. Trace the pattern for the Jacket, making a pattern for the front, with the neck sitting lower and the bottom edge straight, and another for the back with the lower curved bottom edge. Also trace patterns for the Jacket sleeve, Hood gusset, Hood face and Hood side on the web (see page 11), following the lines for the correct size.

2. Press the fabric, arrange it on a flat surface and place the pattern pieces on the fabric so you can cut one back, two fronts, two sleeves, and for the hood, one gusset, one face and two sides. Make sure the grain lines on the pattern are parallel to the selvedge and that any pile runs in the correct direction. Repeat for the lining.

3. Cut two pockets and two elbow patches from contrast fabric.

(CON'T)

> **TIP**
> Add a micro fleece lining to make the jacket really snuggly or a printed cotton lining to make a summer jacket. You can use any of the face templates to create your own little creature.

FACE

1. Using the template on page 207, cut four ears from main fabric, adding 1cm (³/₈in) all around.

2. Prepare the appliqué by backing the fabric for the inner ears and features with adhesive web.

3. Trace the shapes on the paper side and cut out two inner ears, two eyes, a nose and a muzzle.

4. Peeling off the paper backing, arrange the features on the face panel and the inner ears in place, cover with a soft cloth and press into place. Finish by topstitching with matching thread to fix in place.

5. To make the ears, place the front and back right sides together and sew around the curved edges with a 5mm (¹/₄in) seam allowance. Carefully snip around the curve, then turn through and press. Repeat for the second ear.

6. Position and sew the ears into place at the top edge of the face panel.

ASSEMBLING THE HOOD

1. Pin and sew the left and right hood sides to the gusset (or centre panel), right sides together with a 1cm (³/₈in) seam allowance. Press the seams open. Attach the top edge of the face to the front edges of the sides and gusset in the same way, right sides together.

2. Repeat for the hood lining.

3. Place the main hood and lining right sides together and sew all the way around the front edges. Snip into the curved edges as required and turn through.

4. Press, rolling gently to obtain a good finish at the curved edges.

5. Finish by topstitching 5mm (¹/₄in) from the edge all the way around the front edge. See illustration on page 176 for more detail.

MAKING THE POCKETS AND SLEEVE PATCHES

1. Overlock all around the pocket pieces. Turn the top edge back twice by 2cm (³/₄in) and stitch in place. Turn the remaining edges under by 1cm (³/₈in) and press.

2. Cut six triangles of felt for the claws, each 4 × 2cm (1¹/₂ × ³/₄in).

Insert three into position under the edge of each pocket. Pin then sew the pockets into position all the way around 5mm (¹/₄in) from the pressed edge, making sure the claws are trapped into place as you go. Backstitch or reinforce with a small triangle at the start and finish.

3. Cut two oval shapes for the elbow patches, approximately 11 × 13cm (4¹/₄in × 5in). Turn the edges under 5mm (¹/₄in) or overlock. Place one on each sleeve, halfway between the cuff and the top of the back sleeve. Topstitch into place.

WILD THINGS

SEWING TOGETHER

1. Pin the fronts and back right sides together at the shoulders and sew a 1cm (³⁄₈in) seam. Press each seam towards the back of the garment. Topstitch the jacket and seam allowance 5mm (¹⁄₄in) from the seam to strengthen and finish.

2. Working with the jacket flat, pin and sew the sleeves into place, right sides together. Press the seam allowance down towards the sleeve. Topstitch the sleeve and seam allowance 5mm (¹⁄₄in) from the seam to strengthen and finish.

3. Sew the side and sleeve seams and press.

4. Pin the bottom edge of the main hood to the neckline of the jacket, matching notches and allowing the hood to fall short of each front edge on the jacket by 2cm (³⁄₄in) edge. Carefully snip the seam allowance and press.

5. Repeat steps 1–4 for the lining. Turn the lining inside out and position right sides together over the top of the main jacket. Sew the two together around the front of the hood, fronts and hemline, leaving a gap of around 20cm (8in) at the hemline. Carefully cut excess at the front corners, then turn through. Press carefully to give a good finish, then topstitch all around 5mm (¹⁄₄in) from the edge, enclosing the opening at the hemline as you go.

6. To finish the cuffs, carefully press back the lining and main cuff by 1.5cm (5/8in). Align the edges, pin, then topstitch 5mm (¹⁄₄in) from the edge. Press.

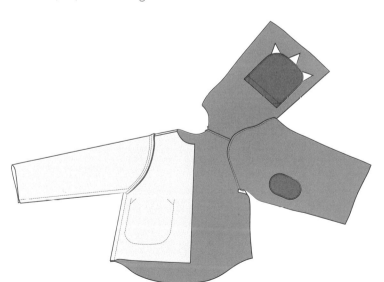

FINISHING

1. Mark the position of the buttonholes from the pattern, and referring to your sewing machine manual, carefully make four buttonholes. (Practise on some layered fabric first, if you want.)

2. Sew the buttons into place.

Bird hoodie

This dynamic hoodie is a great everyday layer, giving a splash of colour at the park. It uses the same template for the face as the owl dress, this time as a tropical bird. Perfect for dress-up and role play. Made from jersey-based fabric, it requires a stretch stitch, so refer to your sewing machine manual for guidance. Generally a zigzag stitch works, offering stretch, followed by overlocking. Test a scrap of fabric before sewing. I've kept it simple too, so there's no need to search for matching ribbed fabric for cuffs or a welt.

YOU WILL NEED

- Hoodie, hoodie sleeve, hood gusset, face and side, and pocket patterns
- 1m (1yd) sweatshirting fabric or fleece, 110cm (44in) or wider
- Tailor's chalk
- Bird face template
- Feather appliqué templates
- Coloured fabrics for the feathers and face features
- Contrast jersey fabric for hood lining (or you can use the main fabric)
- Iron-on, double-sided adhesive web
- Matching sewing threads

CUTTING OUT

1. Choose the best size for your child, using the guide on page 30. Trace the pattern for the Hoodie, making a pattern for the front, with the neck sitting lower and the bottom edge straight, and another for the back with the lower curved bottom edge. Also trace patterns for the Hoodie sleeve, Hoodie pocket, Hoodie face, Hood gusset (or centre panel) and Hood side on the web (see page 11), following the lines for the correct size.

2. Cut one gusset, one face and two sides from the lining fabric. If you are using the main fabric to line the hood then the face panel can be cut with the fabric folded to eliminate the seam at the hood edge.

3. Mark around the pattern pieces using tailor's chalk, adding 1 cm (³⁄₈in) all around. Cut the pieces out carefully.

APPLIQUÉ

1. Prepare appliqué for the body by backing enough contrast fabric with adhesive web for five feathers using the appliqué feather template on page 212. Trace around the shapes on the paper side and cut out. Peeling off the paper backing, position the shapes on the front of the hoodie. Press with a moderate iron to bond.

2. Sew the shapes into place by stitching around the edges.

(CON'T)

3. Prepare the shapes for the face in the same way, using the template on page 212, cutting two beaks and layering circles and crescent shapes for the eyes.

4. Fold the hoodie face panel along the marked lines to create a double semi-circular panel. Alternatively, seam the hood panel with the matching lining piece along the straight edge and fold back.

5. Position the features on the face panel, then press and stitch into place, through the top layer only.

6. Bonding the two beaks together, cut out the diamond and sew around the edges. Set aside for now.

7. Cut two ears from the main fabric using the template on page 212 and sew the straight edges on each, right sides together, to create a cone shape. Snip the excess at the point, turn through and sew into place as marked on the prepared face.

8. Cut 16 underarm feather shapes. Place them in pairs, right sides together and sew around the curved edges. Snip around the curves and turn through.

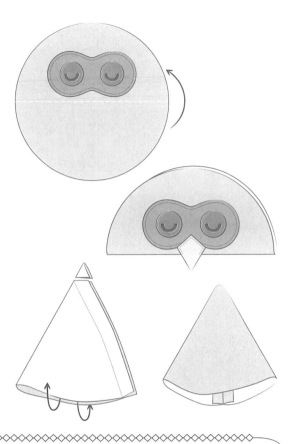

HOOD AND POCKET

1. Pin and sew the left and right sides of the main hood to the gusset, right sides together. Press the seams open. Repeat for the lining.

2. Place the main hood and lining sides together. Pin the curved edge of the face panel between the layers, around the curved front edge of the hood. Sew that seam. Keeping the face panel out of the way, continue to sew the outer edges of the hood together, but leave an opening at the back edge. Turn through the opening and press.

3. Now add the beak to the folded front of the hood. Sew it into place.

4. Prepare the pouch pocket by overlocking all edges. Turn back the two hand hole edges by 2cm (³⁄₄in) and sew. Press back the remaining sides and position on the hoodie. Sew it into place.

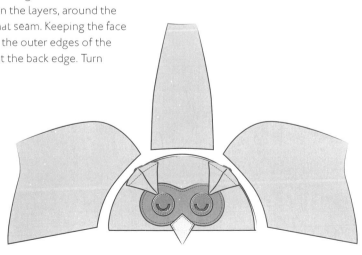

WILD THINGS

SEWING TOGETHER

1. Sew the shoulder seams, right sides together, with a suitable stretch stitch and overlock. Press.

2. Sew the sleeves in place, right sides together and overlock. Press.

3. Overlock the cuff edges.

4. Position four feathers in place along each underarm seam.

5. Sew the side seams, trapping the feathers. Overlock and press.

6. Overlock the hem edge, then turn under by 3cm (1¼in) and stitch with a stretch finish to create a generous hem. Press.

7. Turn back the cuffs by 3cm (1¼in) and stitch as in step 6.

8. Pin and sew the lined hood to the hoodie all around the neckline with a 1cm (³⁄₈in) seam allowance. Overlap the front corners of the hood slightly at the centre front for added strength. Overlock the neck edge. Turn through and press.

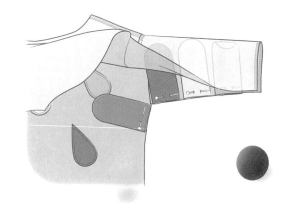

Cat hoodie

This hoodie can be for girls or boys and makes a perfect dress-up costume for Halloween and parties.

YOU WILL NEED

- Hoodie, hoodie sleeve, hood gusset, face and side, and pocket patterns
- 1m (1yd) sweatshirt fabric or fleece, 110cm (44in) or wider
- Tailor's chalk
- Cat face template
- Scraps of fabric for inner ears and face features
- Felt for the claws
- Iron-on, double-sided adhesive web
- Fabric for hood lining (or you can use the main fabric)
- Matching sewing threads

TIP

Made from jersey-based fabric, this garment requires a stretch stitch so refer to your sewing machine manual for guidance. A zigzag stitch works, offering stretch, followed by overlocking. Test a scrap of fabric before sewing. I've kept it simple too, so there's no need to search for matching ribbed fabric for cuffs or a welt.

CUTTING OUT

1. Choose the best size for your child, using the guide on page 30. Trace the pattern for the Hoodie, making a pattern for the front, with the neck sitting lower and the bottom edge straight, and another for the back with the lower curved bottom edge. Also trace patterns for the Hoodie sleeve, Hoodie face, Hood gusset, Hood side and pocket on the web (see page 11), following the lines for the correct size.

2. Press the fabric, arrange it on a flat surface and place the pattern pieces on the fabric so you can cut one back, one front, two sleeves, two pockets and, for the hood, one gusset, one face (cut two placed on a folded edge as shown in the pattern) and two sides. Make sure the grain lines on the pattern are parallel to the selvedge and any pile runs in the correct direction. Cut just one gusset and two sides for the hood lining.

3. Mark around the pattern pieces using tailor's chalk, adding 1cm (³/₈in) all around. Cut the pieces out carefully.

(CON'T)

ADDING DETAIL

1. Using the template on page 206, prepare the face features by bonding the coloured fabrics to adhesive web, tracing the shapes on the paper backing and cutting out.

2. Peeling off the paper backing, position the shapes on the face piece, then fuse with a moderate iron and stitch to secure. Fold the face panel along the marked lines to create a panel.

3. Cut four cat ears from the main fabric and two inner ears from pink or contrast fabric bonded to adhesive web. Peeling off the backing, bond the contrast inner pieces to the centres of two of the main ear pieces. Pin each ear front to an ear back, right sides together and sew around the curved edges, leaving the bottom open. Carefully trim back the fabric from the pointed edge, turn the ear through, and press. Sew the ears into place as marked on the face panel.

HOOD AND POCKET

1. Pin and sew the left and right sides of the main hood to the gusset, right sides together. Press the seams open. Repeat for the lining.

2. Place the main hood and lining sides together. Pin the curved edge of the face panel between the layers, around the curved front edge of the hood. Sew that seam. Keeping the face panel out of the way, continue to sew the outer edges of the hood together, but leaving an opening in the back edge. Turn through the opening and press.

3. Prepare the pockets by overlocking all the edges. Turn back the two hand hole edges by 2cm (¾in) and sew. Press back the remaining sides and position on the hoodie. Cut six triangles of felt for claws, each 4 × 2cm (1½ × ¾in). Insert three in position under each pocket. Sew the pockets into place, trapping the claws into position as you go.

SEWING TOGETHER

1. Sew the shoulder seams, right sides together, with a suitable stretch stitch and overlock. Press.

2. Sew the sleeves in place, right sides together and overlock. Press.

3. Overlock the cuff edges.

4. Sew the side seams.

5. Overlock the hem edge, then turn under by 3cm (1¼in) and stitch with a stretch finish to create a generous hem. Press.

6. Turn back the cuffs by 3cm (1¼in) and stitch as in step 5.

7. Pin and sew the lined hood to the hoodie all around the neckline with a 1cm (³⁄₈in) seam allowance. Overlap the front corners of the hood slightly at the centre front for added strength. Overlock the neck edge. Turn through and press.

Mouse hat

This little character hat is simple to sew and makes a
perfect baby gift. Try spot or printed ears in soft colours.

YOU WILL NEED

- ⊕ Hat face, side and gusset
  patterns
- ⊕ Mouse template
- ⊕ 50cm (20in) square of fabric
- ⊕ 50cm (20in) square of lining
  fabric
- ⊕ Tailor's chalk (optional)
- ⊕ Black fabric for face features
- ⊕ Pink fabric for the ears and
  nose
- ⊕ Iron-on, double-sided
  adhesive web
- ⊕ Matching sewing threads

CUTTING OUT

1. Choose the best size for your child, using the guide below. Trace
the patterns for the Hat face, Hat gusset and Hat side in the envelope,
following the lines for the correct size.

2. Press the fabric, arrange it on a flat surface and place the pattern
pieces on the fabric so you can cut one gusset, one face and two sides.
Make sure the grain lines on the pattern are parallel to the selvedge and
that any pile runs in the correct direction. Repeat for the lining.

3. Mark around the pattern pieces using tailor's chalk, adding 1cm (³/₈in)
all around. Cut the pieces out carefully.

SIZE GUIDE

Size	Age
XS	6 months
S	1–2 years
M	3–5 years
L	5–7 years

FACE

1. Using the template on page 206, cut out four ears from the main
fabric, adding 1cm (³/₈in) all around.

2. Prepare the appliqué by backing the fabric for the inner ears and
features with adhesive web.

(CON'T)

3. Trace the shapes onto the paper side, then cut out two inner ears, two eyes, a nose and six whiskers.

4. Peeling off the paper backing, arrange the features on the face panel and the inner ears on the two ear pieces, cover with a soft cloth and press into place. Stitch in place with matching thread.

5. To make the ears, place an ear front and back right sides together and sew 5mm (¼in) from the curved edges. Carefully snip the curved edges to create a smooth finish. Turn through, press, and repeat for the second ear.

6. Position and sew the ears into place on the top edge of the face panel.

ASSEMBLING THE HAT

1. Pin and sew the left and right hat sides to the gusset (centre panel), right sides together, with a 1cm (³⁄₈in) seam allowance. Press the seams open. Attach the top edge of the face to the front edges of the sides and gusset in the same way, right sides together.

2. Repeat for the lining.

3. Cut six triangles of felt for claws, each 4 × 2cm (1½ × ¾in). Insert three in position under the end of each ear flap.

4. Place the main hat and lining right sides together and sew all the way around, leaving approximately 8cm (3in) open at the centre back. Snip into the curved edges as required and turn through.

5. Press, rolling gently to obtain a good finish at the curved edges.

6. Finish by topstitching 5mm (¼in) from the edge all the way around, at the same time closing the opening.

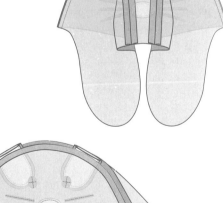

WILD THINGS

Badger hat

This hat is a great project to try before the dresses and dungarees as the pieces are smaller and easier to handle. The hats make perfect gifts and the larger size may even fit you too!

YOU WILL NEED

- Hat face, side and gusset patterns
- Badger template
- 50cm (20in) square of fabric
- 50cm (20in) square of lining fabric
- Tailor's chalk
- Contrast black and white fabric for the face
- Black and grey fabric for the face features and ears
- Pink fabric for the ear inners
- White felt for the claws
- Iron-on, double-sided adhesive web
- Matching sewing threads

CUTTING OUT

1. Choose the best size for your child, using the guide below. Trace the patterns for the Hat face, Hat gusset and Hat side in the envelope, following the lines for the correct size.

2. Press the main and black fabrics, arrange them on a flat surface and place the pattern pieces on the fabric so you can cut one gusset and two sides from the main fabric and one face from the black fabric. Make sure the grain lines on the pattern are parallel to the selvedge and that any pile runs in the correct direction. Repeat, cutting out all the pieces in the lining fabric.

3. Mark around the pattern pieces using tailor's chalk, adding 1cm (3/8in) all around. Cut the pieces out carefully.

(CON'T)

SIZE GUIDE	
Size	**Age**
XS	6 months
S	1–3 years
M	3–5 years
L	5–7 years

FACE

1. Using the template on page 213, cut out four ears from the black fabric, adding 1cm (³/₈in) all around.

2. Using the template, cut two white face stripes, adding 1cm (³/₈in) to the edges. Turn the long edges under by 1cm (³/₈in) and press. Position them onto the face panel and topstitch the edges to secure.

3. Prepare the appliqué by backing the fabric for the nose, eyes and inner ears with adhesive web.

4. Trace the shapes onto the paper side, then cut out two inner ears, two eyes and a nose.

5. Peeling off the paper backing, arrange the features on the face panel and the inner ears on two ear pieces, cover with a soft cloth and press into place. Topstitch in place using matching sewing thread.

6. To make the ears, place an ear front and back right sides together and sew around the curved edge with a 5mm (¹/₄in) seam allowance. Carefully snip the curved edges to create a smooth finish. Turn through, press, and repeat for the second ear.

7. Position and sew the ears into place on the top edge of the face panel.

ASSEMBLING THE HAT

1. Pin and sew the left and right hat sides to the gusset (centre panel), right sides together, with a 1cm (³/₈in) seam allowance. Press the seams open. Attach the top edge of the face to the front edges of the sides and gusset in the same way, right sides together.

2. Repeat for the lining.

3. Cut six triangles of felt for claws, each 4 × 2cm (1¹/₂ × ³/₄in). Insert three in position under the end of each ear flap.

4. Place the main hat and lining right sides together and sew all the way around, leaving approximately 8cm (3in) open at the centre back. Snip into the curved edges as required and turn through.

5. Press, rolling gently to obtain a good finish at the curved edges.

6. Finish by topstitching 5mm (¹/₄in) from the edge all the way around, at the same time as closing the opening.

Templates

RAINBOW APPLIQUÉ

Increase by 150%
Cut on the fold

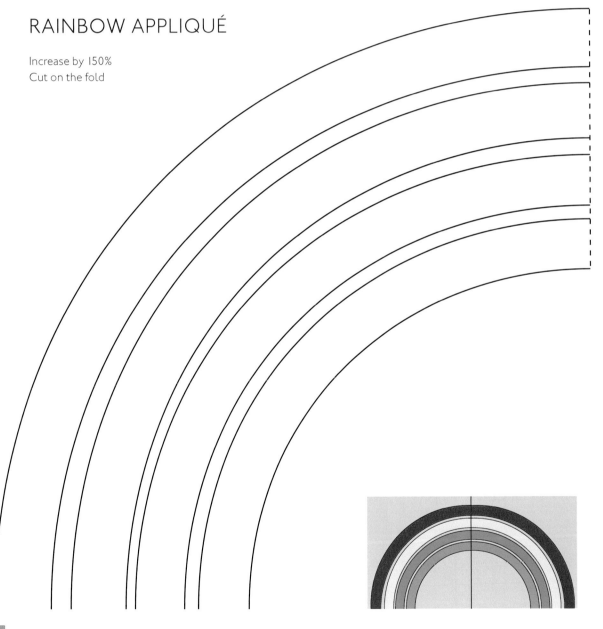

FLOWER POT APPLIQUÉ

Increase by 200%

LANDSCAPE APPLIQUÉ

Increase by 150%

SEASIDE APPLIQUÉ

Increase by 150%

BABY BUNTING APPLIQUÉ

Use at 100%

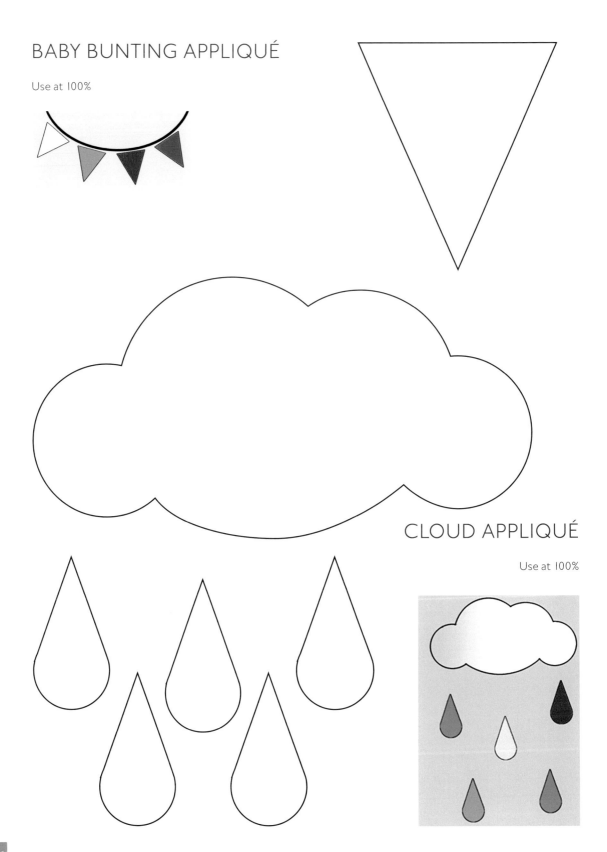

CLOUD APPLIQUÉ

Use at 100%

SUNSHINE APPLIQUÉ

Increase by 150%

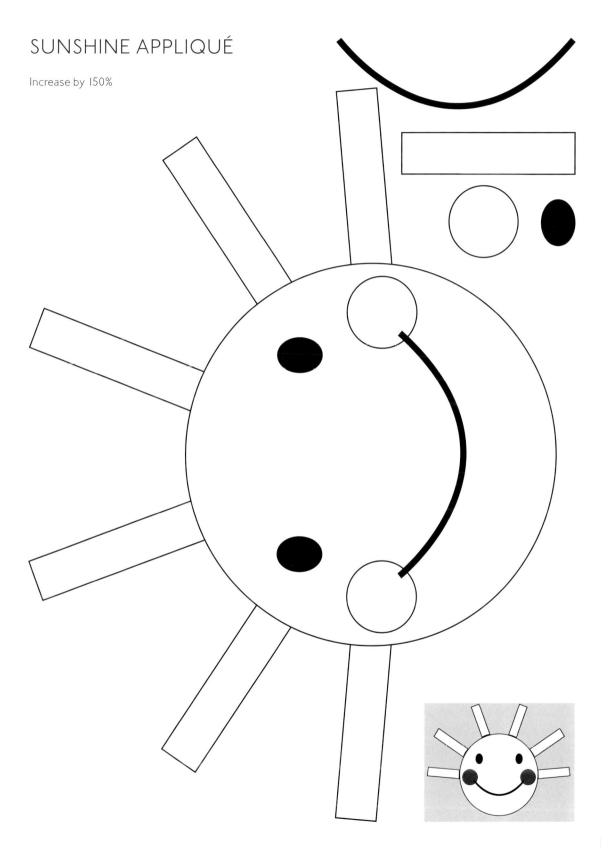

KITE APPLIQUÉ

Use at 100%

FOX/WOLF FACE APPLIQUÉ

Increase by 150%
Cut out the ear pieces and face
panels with 1cm (³/₈in) seam
allowance all around

LITTLE CHICK FACE APPLIQUÉ

Increase by 150%
Cut out the webbed feet
with 1cm (³/₈in) seam
allowance all around

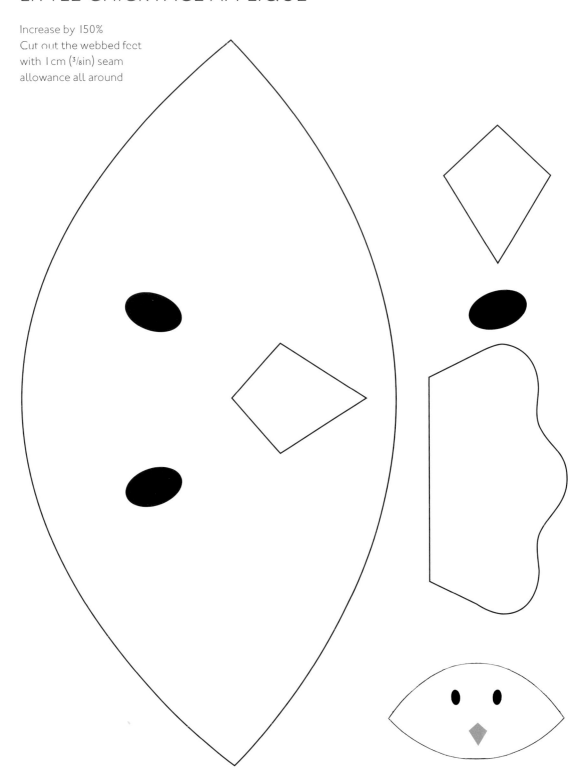

OWL FACE APPLIQUÉ

Increase by 150%
Cut out the ears with 1cm (³/₈in)
seam allowance all around

MOUSE/CAT FACE APPLIQUÉ

Increase by 150%
Cut out the ears with 1 cm (³⁄₈in)
seam allowance all around

BEAR FACE APPLIQUÉ

Increase by 150%

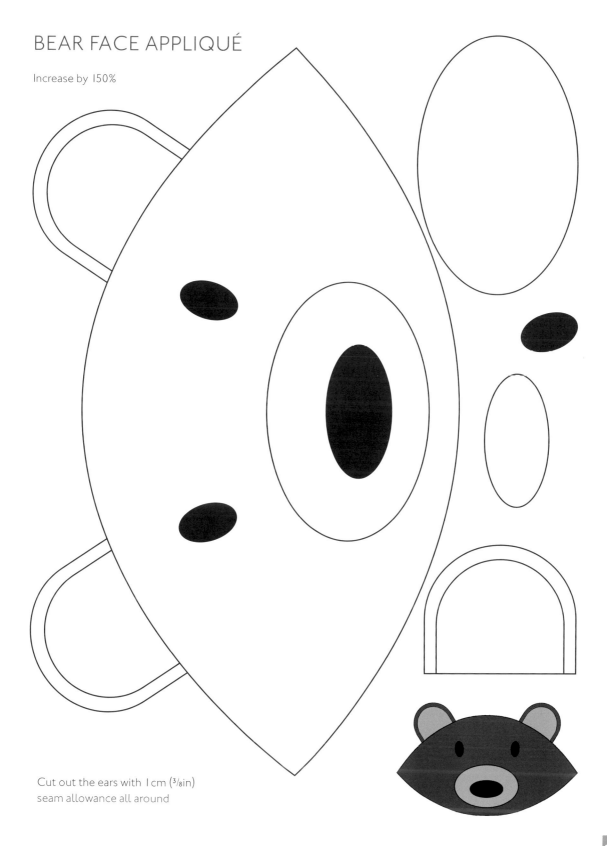

Cut out the ears with 1cm (³⁄₈in)
seam allowance all around

PUPPY
FACE
APPLIQUÉ

Increase by 150%
Cut out the ears with
1 cm (³/₈in) seam allowance
all around

SUNSHINE APPLIQUÉ

Increase by 150%

Small cloud

RAINBOW APPLIQUÉ

Increase by 150%

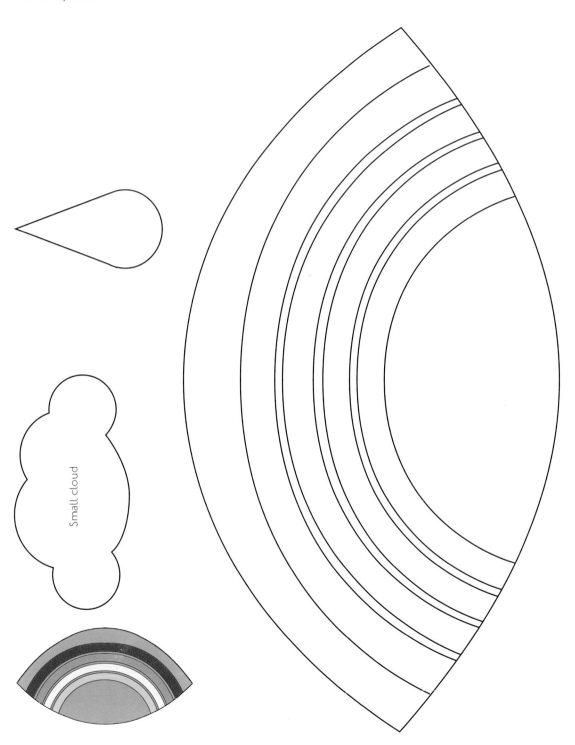

Small cloud

WILD THINGS

LION FACE APPLIQUÉ

Increase by 150%
Cut out the ears with 1cm (³⁄₈in)
seam allowance all around

BIRD FACE APPLIQUÉ

Increase by 150%
Cut out the underarm feathers
with 1 cm (³⁄₈in) seam allowance
all around

Underarm feather

Appliqué feather

BADGER FACE APPLIQUÉ

Increase by 150%
Cut out the ears and face stripes
with 1 cm (³⁄₈in) seam allowance
all around

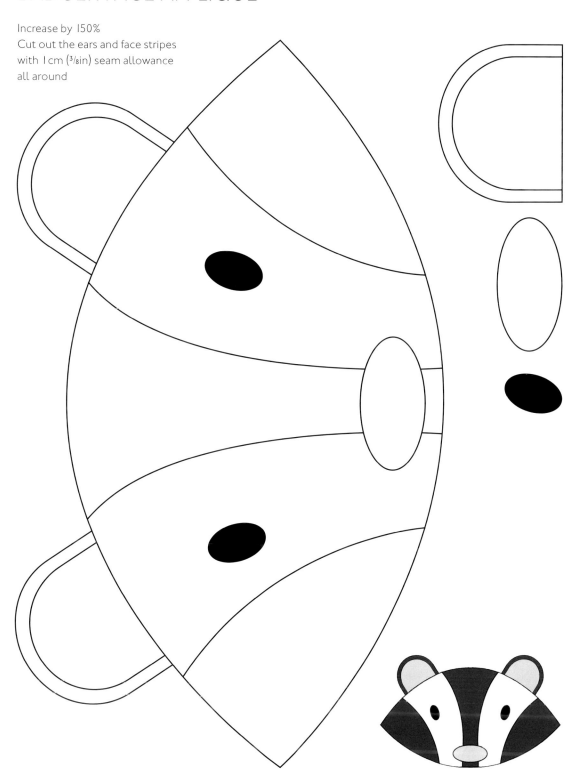

Glossary

Appliqué
This term comes from the French word for 'to apply'. In sewing terms, to apply shape and pattern using one fabric to another.

Backstitch
Also known as reverse stitching, this provides extra durability at the start and end of a seam or line of stitching.

Baste
To roughly join together two fabrics or layers before sewing. Sewing threads are removed later. Also known as tacking.

Bias
Fabric cut on the bias is cut at a 45-degree angle to the selvedge or finished fabric edge.

Binding
This is the technique of creating a decorative border to finish an edge, using pre-prepared or self-made fabric, often bias-binding.

Blindstitch
A stitch often used on a garment hem that is invisible, achieved by working against a folded edge, carefully catching or picking the edge of the fold with the needle and sewing so that the thread is concealed.

Ease
Gently allowing one longer seam to match another when sewing, by 'easing' into place, usually when sewing curved or gathered edges.

Edge stitching
Stitching close to an edge to secure appliqué or provide a neat finish.

Fat quarter
A fat quarter refers to a quarter yard of quilting fabric, often quilter's cotton, measuring 45cm (18in) × 55cm (22in), assuming that the fabric is 110cm (44in) wide. Refer to each project for required fabric quantities or to the measurements of the child, which are given in both metric and imperial measurements.

Finish
Overall presentation and appearance, achieved with good practice and careful handle, especially through pressing. Refers also to a treatment of a fabric such as a coating or brush 'finish'.

Face
Refers to the top, correct, or 'right side' of the fabric.

Facing
This is an inner layer of fabric, cut to form a finished edge and strengthen the main body of a garment.

French seam
A seam in which all raw edges are trapped by sewing twice.

Fold line
Refers to a marking on a pattern that requires you to place the pattern on to a folded piece of fabric, when the opposite side of the folded area is symmetrical.

Gather
Easing, or runching, one fabric to another to create a gathered finish.

Grain line
The grain line is marked on the pattern piece as a long arrow, normally parallel to the centre front or centre back of the garment. It indicates where to place the pattern on the fabric.

Hems
The lower edge of a garment that requires hand or machine stitching to finish.

Notch
A marking on a pattern piece that denotes where it, and a corresponding notch on another pattern piece, are intended to be placed together, rather like a jigsaw puzzle.

Overlock
A specific machine stitch that will finish and trim simultaneously to eliminate raw edges.

Pile or nap
Refers to fabrics with a raised pile such as velvet or corduroy, which have a clear direction to the way the pile lies, meaning you will need to cut everything with the pile running in the same direction.

Pressing
Use of a good-quality steam iron, to prepare and finish a garment, often 'pressing' seams open.

Raw edge
This is the unfinished edge of cut fabric.

Right sides together / RS facing
This refers to when the face or right sides of the fabrics are placed together before sewing.

Rouleau loop
A loop made from bias-cut fabric, used to loop around a button to form a fastening.

Seam
A seam is made when two fabrics are sewn with edges together.

Seam allowance
The additional fabric between the sewing line and the edge of the fabric.

Satin stitch
A flush smooth finish created by sewing back and forth close together along an edge. Can be used to hand sew buttonholes.

Selvedge
Refers to the finished edge of the fabric running along the warp of a woven fabric.

Snipping curves
Cutting into curved seam allowances to create a better finish and reduce bulk.

Tack or baste
Hand sewing to temporarily secure layers in place, which helps with fine work. Tacking threads are removed after sewing.

Topstitch
Topstitching can be used for decorative purposes but more often it is used to achieve a flat and strong edge finish. Often in a contrast colour.

Understitch
Strengthens and neatens edges. Rather than topstitch, understitching cannot be seen from the face of the garment . Sew close to the edge on the inside of the garment with all seam allowances pressed to the inside of the garment.

Warp
In woven fabrics, runs lengthways parallel to the selvedge.

Weft
In woven fabrics, runs widthways at 45-degrees to the selvedge.

Wrong side
Refers to the reverse, back, or 'wrong side' of the fabric.

Zigzag stitch
A stitch setting that moves the needle from left to right rather than in a straight line. Can be used to neaten a raw edge where an overlock is not available, or to create a stretch stitch.

Index

A

appliqué 16–17, 50, 64, 86, 98,
    160, 182
    baby bunting template 200
    badger face template 213
    bear face template 207
    bird face template 212
    flower pot template 197
    fox face template 203
    kite template 202
    landscape template 198
    lion face template 211
    little chick template 204
    mouse face template 206
    owl face template 205
    puppy face template 208
    rainbow template 196
    seaside template 199
    sunshine template 201
    sunshine/rainbow templates
        209–210
    wolf face template 203
aprons 100–103

B

babies
    baby knickers 118
    baby sun set 92–95
    bonnet 173
back openings
    keyhole 40
    simple 70
    zipped 41, 70
backstitch 18
bib tops 161
binding 19
bottom patches 127, 151,
    155, 167
bunting 74, 89, 117
buttonholes 21
buttons 20

C

cape, fairy-tale 168–171
clothing sizes 30–32
collars 59, 68, 75
cuffs, ankle 78
cutting 21

D

designs see garment designs
dresses
    baby bunting sundress 89–91
    baby mouse 144–147
    baby sun set 92–95
    carousel 72–75
    flower collar 57–60
    flower pot pinafore 52–55
    fox 131–134
    happy landscape 62–65
    little chick 136–139
    little house apron 97–99
    Little Missy 67–71

    little painter artist smock
        105–109
    owl 141–143
    'pillowcase' top 91
    rainbow 49–51
    reversible pinny with pockets
        44–47
    seaside sundress 84–87
    simple A-line 37–42
dressmaker's pins 8
dungarees see trousers

E

easing 21

F

fabric loops 40
fabric straps 84, 87, 94, 98, 103, 134,
    139, 143, 147, 151, 156, 164
fabric ties 76, 82, 90, 100

fabrics
    bias 18
    cutting 21
    easing 21
    fat quarter 22
    finish 22
    grain lines 24
    knitted 12
    online suppliers 12
    pile or nap 25
    raw edge 25
    selvedge 26
    stretch 12
    velvet 171
    woven 12
facings 22, 67, 74
    contrast 109, 151, 156
fat quarter 22
finishing 11, 22, 33
French seams 22

G

garment designs
baby bunting sundress 89–91
baby knickers 118
baby mouse dress 144–147
baby sun set 92–95
badger hat 193–195
bear jacket 179–181
bird hoodie 182–185
bloomers 121–122
bonnet 173
bumblebee shortie romper
    81–83
carousel dress 72–75
carousel skirt 115–117
cat hoodie 187–189
fairy-tale cape 168–171
flower apron 103
flower collar dress 57–60
flower pot pinafore 52–55
fox dress 131–134
funky romper 76–79
happy landscape dress 62–65
little chick dress 136–139
little helper apron 100–103
little house apron dress 97–99

Little Missy dress 67–71
little painter artist smock
    105–109
mouse hat 190–192
Mr Bear dungarees 148–151
Mr Wolf dungarees 163–167
owl dress 141–143
puppy dog dungarees 153–156
rainbow dress 49–51
reversible pinny with pockets
    44–47
reversible pull-ons 124–127
seaside sundress 84–87
simple A-line dress 37–42
sleepy lion jacket 174–177
star apron 103
sunshine/rainbow dungarees
    158–161
windy day kite skirt 112–114
gathering 24

H

hand openings 171
hats
    see also hoods
    badger 193–195
    mouse 190–192
hems 24
    contrast turnbacks 167
    elasticated 83
    scalloped 117
hoods 168, 173, 176, 180, 184, 188
    see also hats

I

iron and ironing board 8, 25

J

jackets
    bear 179–181
    bird hoodie 182–185
    cat hoodie 187–189
    sleepy lion 174–177

K

knickers
    baby 118
    bloomers 121–122

M

measuring child 30

O

online
    fabric suppliers 12
    ideas and inspiration 13

P

pattern cutting square 8
patterns
    fold lines 22
    grain lines 24
'pillowcase' dress top 91
pockets
    animal/bird feet 133, 139, 142,
        146, 150, 165, 176, 180, 188
    contrast top 133
    contrasting 38, 76
    gathered top 50, 78, 94, 142
    large 98, 100, 106, 142
    motif decoration 46
    patch 100
    pouch 106, 142, 184
pressing and finishing 11

Q

quilter's cottons 12

R

rompers
    bumblebee shortie romper
        81–83

funky romper 76–79
rouleau loop 26

S

scissors 8
seam ripper 8
seams 26
sewing kit 8
sewing machine 8
    learning to use 11
    stretch fabrics 12
sewing needles 8
shoulder straps 87, 94, 134, 139,
    143, 147, 151, 156, 164
skirts
    carousel 115–117
    windy day kite 112–114
sleeve patches 176, 180
stitching
    backstitch 18
    edges 22
    tacking and basting 27
    topstitch 27, 42

T

tailor's chalk 8
tape measure 8
techniques
    appliqué 16–17, 50, 64, 86, 98,
      160, 182
    backstitch 18
    binding 19
    buttonholes 21
    buttons 20
    clothing sizes 30–32
    curved edges and corners 26
    cutting 21
    easing 21
    edge stitching 22
    facing 22
    finishing 11, 22
    fold lines 22
    French seams 22
    gathering 24
    grain lines 24

hems 24
joining gathered skirts 114
keyhole back openings 40
measuring child 30
pile or nap 25
pockets 38, 46, 50, 54, 139
pressing 11, 25
raw edge 25
right sides together 26
rouleau loop 26
seams 26
selvedge 26
tacking and basting 27
topstitch 27, 42
zips 29, 41, 70
templates
    baby bunting appliqué 200
    badger face appliqué 213
    bear face appliqué 207
    bird face appliqué 212
    flower pot appliqué 197
    fox face appliqué 203
    kite appliqué 202
    landscape appliqué 198
    lion face appliqué 211
    little chick appliqué 204
    mouse face appliqué 206
    owl face appliqué 205
    puppy face appliqué 208
    rainbow appliqué 196
    seaside appliqué 199
    sunshine appliqué 201
    sunshine/rainbow appliqué
      209–210
    wolf face appliqué 203
trimming
    animal/bird ears 146, 155, 183,
      188, 192, 195
    animal/bird faces 133, 139, 142,
      146, 150, 155, 164, 174, 179,
      182–184, 188
    animal/bird feet 133, 139, 142,
      146, 150, 165, 176, 180
    appliqué 16–17, 50, 64, 86, 98,
      160, 182
    binding 19
    bird beak 184
    bird feathers 184
    bottom patches 127, 151, 155, 167

bunting 74, 89, 117
buttonholes 21
buttons 20
contrast facings 109, 151, 156
contrast pockets 38
contrast topstitching 42
contrast turning 47
flower collar 59
gathered top pockets 50, 78,
    94, 142
hand openings 171
motif decoration 46, 58, 68
recycling old scraps 11
scalloped hems 117
sleeve patches 176, 180
trousers
    Mr Bear dungarees 148–151
    Mr Wolf dungarees 163–167
    puppy dog dungarees 153–156
    reversible pull-ons 124–127
    sunshine/rainbow dungarees
      158–161

W

workspace 11

Y

yokes 76–79, 82–83, 90, 160

Z

zips 29, 41, 70

Stockists

Remember to always shop local whenever you can!

FOR CORDUROY, AND WILD THINGS EXCLUSIVE FABRICS
www.wildthingsdresses.com
www.wildthingstosew.com

FOR A COOL SELECTION OF THE BEST QUILTER'S COTTONS
Fancy Moon: www.fancymoon.co.uk
Fabric Rehab: http://fabricrehab.co.uk
Seamstar: http://www.seamstar.co.uk

PRINT HOUSES:
Review their ranges and buy from your local retailer
Michael Miller Fabrics: www.michaelmillerfabrics.com
Alexander Henry Fabrics: www.ahfabrics.com

FOR BEAUTIFUL CONTEMPORARY WOVEN AND JERSEY PRINTS
Monaluna: www.monaluna.com

FOR TRIMS AND SUPPLIES
Etsy.com: www.etsy.com/uk/browse/craft-supplies
Barnyarns: www.barnyarns.co.uk

MACHINES
Brother Sewing Machnes: www.brothersewing.co.uk

Acknowledgements

Thank you to Clare Hulton who believed in my creative vision, and introduced me to Amanda Harris and Jillian Young, and their brilliant team at Orion Publishing, as well as designer Gemma Wilson and illustrator Kuo Kang Chen, who shared the vision to make this happen. To the creatively wonderful Kat Goldin who first sowed the seed to my becoming an author. Thank you to Will Shaddock and Jenny Murdoch for ingenious photography and styling, and working magic with their clear-sighted vision, chilled outlook, and great taste.

To Linda Young and apprentice Drew, the skilled production backbone to Wild Things, and for bringing UK production back to her native Scotland. To Michelle and Seema, for keeping things running every day, and to Maria and Rachel Midgeley, and Inge Wolfenden for their sewing expertise. Thanks to my supportive suppliers, especially Debbie Wilson and Lynsey Beaton and Becky at Peanut and Pip, who understand that you have to start small to grow something big.

To the dedicated teams at Etsy and Notonthehighst.com for helping me grow. For my online friends and mentors including photographer Jenni Närväinen.

To my little muses Silva and Lila, and models, Charley, Dio, Llords and Evie.

Most importantly to my family: to Sandra, my mum, and rainbow cake baker, who introduced me at an early age to sewing, with unfailing support. To sisters Cara and events manager Ceri, and Adam for keeping my spirits high and believing in me.

To warm friends and fellow makers of Brinscall, especially Hayley and Sorrel, for working the 'old school' way; Carol for her wit, and Kirsty for loaning her gorgeous children to model. And also to Katie and Karl, Caroline and Paul for carrying me through the journey, and Alex and Lisa for teenage Saturdays spent fabric hunting and sewing before the big night ahead.

And finally, thank you to Gary, my partner, for endless encouragement and support, and being the craziest dad for our children, feeding their minds with his love of literature and storytelling.

CREDITS

Will Shaddock and
Jenny Murdoch :
www.willshaddock.co.uk

Jennifer Moore at
Monaluna

Natalie for shoes at
Livie and Luca
www.livieandluca.co.uk

Brother Sewing Machines
Europe
GmbH – UK Branch
www.brothersewing.co.uk

First published in Great Britain in 2015
by Weidenfeld & Nicolson,
an imprint of The Orion Publishing Group Ltd

10 9 8 7 6 5 4 3 2 1

Orion House
Upper St Martin's Lane
London WC2H 9EA
An Hachette UK Company

Text © Kirsty Hartley 2015
Design and layout copyright © Weidenfeld & Nicolson 2015

Designer: Gemma Wilson
Photographer: Will Shaddock
Prop stylist: Jenny Murdoch
Illustrator: Kuo Kang Chen
Project editor: Jillian Young
Copy editor: Clare Sayer
Proofreader: Karen Hemingway
Indexer: Cherry Ekins

All rights reserved. No part of this publication may be reproduced,
stored in a retrieval system, or transmitted, in any form or by any
means, electronic, mechanical, photocopying, recording or otherwise,
without the prior permission of both the copyright owner and the above
publisher.

The right of Kirsty Hartley to be identified as the author of this work has
been asserted in accordance with the Copyright, Designs and Patents
Act 1988.

A CIP catalogue record for this book is available from the British Library.

ISBN: 978 0 2978 7125 5

Printed in China

The Orion Publishing Group's policy is to use papers that are natural,
renewable and recyclable and made from wood grown in sustainable
forests. The logging and manufacturing processes are expected to
conform to environmental regulations of the country of origin.

www.orionbooks.co.uk